Revi

The Bridge to Heaven

Interviews with
MARIA ESPERANZA
of BETANIA

by

DREW J. MARIANI

and

MICHAEL H. BROWN

Betania Publications

In the United States
One Marian Way
Medway, MA 02053
[508]533-5377
[508]533-2877 (Fax)
mariancommunity.org

In Venezuela
[58-212] 963-7264
mariaesperanza.org

Published by Marian Communications, Ltd., 1993
Published by Queenship Publishing Company, 2003
Published by Betania Publication, 2006

Library of Congress Number: 2003091198

ISBN: 1-57918-233-X

Betania Publications

In the United States
One Marian Way
Medway, MA 02053
[508]533-5377
[508]533-2877 (Fax)
mariancommunity.org

In Venezuela
[58-212] 963-7264
mariaesperanza.org

Table of Contents

DEDICATION

It is with hearts filled with love and gratitude that this book is dedicated to the memory of Mrs. Maria Esperanza Medrano de Bianchini ~ visionary, mystic, and the messenger of "Mary, Virgin, and Mother Reconciler of all People and Nations."

Mrs. Maria Esperanza de Bianchini was born on November 22, 1928 and died on August 7, 2004. She surrendered her life to evangelize and to educate youth and families according to the doctrine of the Roman Catholic Church. Maria Esperanza loved her Church.

Maria Esperanza de Bianchini loved her own family but also opened her home and heart to all people from every walk of life who came to visit and pray with her.

Maria Esperanza, your spiritual children give thanks to God for you and remember you in our prayers, always calling to mind your faith and love.

Acknowledgments

This book would not have been possible without Drew Mariani and Debbie Reader of Marian Communications in Lima, Pennsylvania. Their dedication to the cause of spreading Our Lady's legitimate messages is palpable. Special thanks to Pamela Tyrrell for conceiving the idea for this book and also for transcription. For help in translation: Ya Ya Cantu, Kathy Chebly, and Bridget Hylak-Hooker (Come Alive Communications). May they be blessed. I'd also like to thank Geo and Maria, along with all their children and in-laws, for providing time during hectic schedules. Likewise are regards extended to all those who consented to interviews, often courageously so, especially Bishop Pio Bello Ricardo. My thanks to Lois Malik for taking me on my first visit to Betania. God's peace!

For this new edition, we owe special thanks to Joe Febo, Ron and Charlene Kyle, Carlos Marrero Bornn, John Crimi and Paul Miller. May God bless you richly!

Prologue

The book that follows is in large part a book we released in the early 1990s on Venezuelan mystic Maria Esperanza. We have since updated it and are re-releasing it because it's highly pertinent — and is the only extensive series of interviews with her available. We have re-interviewed Maria to bring it up to speed, and we hope you benefit from some of her new and in some cases dramatic insights.

As Maria has long prophesied, it is both an exciting and dangerous time. She always sees matters in a positive light (the Light of Jesus) and she emphasizes that whatever does occur in the future will be a "purification," a clearing way of debris, a cleansing. That means it will be followed by better times. But the question becomes what will occur on the *way* to those brighter times — and how we can pray and work to make the road safer.

We revisit the words of Maria Esperanza Bianchini in the wake of the war on terror and September 11. It is a different time, and Maria prophesied it. On December 9, 1992, Maria told a group of visiting Americans that she saw "two huge towers with black smoke all around them." She had said they were in New York and asked pilgrims to pray about it. Something was going to happen in America, she said — *and indeed, a couple months later, on February 26, 1993, there was the first terrorist bombing at the World Trade Center.*

Seven years later, in December of 2000, in the waning moment of that year, the headline on our website, www.spiritdaily.com, was: "World-known mystic Maria Esperanza warns U.S. of foreign danger, sees world 'saddened' in a short while, is concerned with the Mid-East, the Pope, and two nations." More precisely, Maria was warning about two foreign "powers," one that she described as small, the other larger, acting in such a way as to provoke America. "The United States has to be very careful," she warned. "It has to act with a lot of prudence." As her son-in-law, Carlos Marrero Bornn, explained to us at the time (ten months before September 11), "She feels in her heart that there is a certain big thing that is about to happen." Carlos went on to say that a heaviness in her chest indicated something was on the way.

Maria, whose visions are associated with the apparition site of Betania near Caracas — one of the few such sites winning formal Church recognition during the twentieth century — said that matters would unfold in the way of a series of events climaxed by a major situation. She said that the next several years would be crucial, and that the U.S. had to be "very, very alert."

"The United States must take care of itself a lot because there is much hatred toward the U.S. right now, so now *more than ever* the United States must be careful," admonished the great mystic. "There are two nations that have their eyes on the U.S. right now. They are not necessarily big nations. One is very smart and powerful and the other is less [so] and these two nations are in accordance and will be allies. They want somehow to upset the United States, *to work inside* and cause disturbances. They feel they can put the nation in jeopardy working not just from the outside but also from the inside... *They have people inside already...*" [my emphasis]

And so it was. At the time, in those days that seem so innocent in retrospect, Esperanza was foreseeing something that would be sent "as a sign, as an awakening of consciences," a very big event. "Something that will shake the world," said Marrero, who functions as her expert translator. "She feels it is going to take a little more time — not too much time, but a little more... Not right now. A little further than now."

As I said, that was toward the end of December 2000. The timing was expressed in a way that appears highly accurate in retrospect. She specifically warned about materialism — and of course when the event came it involved the very epicenter of Western materialism. The following March, while visiting New Jersey, Maria warned that evils like human cloning were going to lead to unfortunate events. A couple months after, she told her family that the upheavals in Israel and natural stirrings such as the volcanoes (at the time, in places like the Philippines and Italy) were "specific signs" that events were intensifying and that in the next several years they would join to precipitate a major occurrence.

If *that* wasn't enough, on August 25, at 9:35 p.m., those close to Maria recorded her as saying that "a great event will be happening in three weeks or three months. As the Holy Father's condition weakens, the event is for the whole world."

When September 11 did happen, Maria turned out to be in the New York City area on another visit! Soon after, reports came that the Pope was failing; true to Maria's prophecy, the Pope seemed to be weakening. "His hands trembled, he slumped in his chair and aides rushed to his side to offer comfort halfway through a speech he could not finish," said *The Washington Post*. "Pope John Paul II's stop in Armenia on Tuesday, his fourth day of a foreign tour, offered a new test of the 81-year-old pontiff's frail health."

Maria had been telling family and friends that she was herself suffering in order to take some of the burden off the Pope and soon was being treated for an ailment that mimicked the Pope's. She became stooped, often hunched over, and had great difficulty (and still does) walking and even talking. Incredibly, Maria began to suffer symptoms of what some diagnosed as a manifestation of Parkinson's!

But none of this derailed her insights, and her mind remained sharp. The day after the World Trade Center collapsed, Esperanza told *Spirit Daily* there was a "roaring lion" behind the terrorism. Later it was learned that the name "Osama" means "roaring lion"!

At this point, let us make clear that Maria doesn't like to

speak of these things, nor to display her talents. She is circumspect. She never draws attention to herself. But she has granted permission to quote some of her remarks and her missive is important at this present hour. Her message: pray for the Pope, because he's especially in need. Pray for the Church. Pray for the United States. She has warned that the world is going through "convulsions" and that the U.S. remains acutely vulnerable despite relatively sedate periods since September 11. "The risk is still there," she says. "You have to be alert all the time because there may be surprises. *The United States must be very careful right now.*"

In other words, although hopeful that certain events would be averted, Maria's concern has not lessened since September 11. "There is a group of people who are trying to show the world that things are under control, but if we do not unite in prayer things will get worse," she says. "The only way to see the truth is through humility. We have to be very humble, because pride is what is destroying the world, and so is materialism. We must be humble and generous. The people must be united because these are very difficult times. We are living in a very difficult time. Mankind is going too fast and is not stopping to meditate. There are those making decisions without really meditating, in their own way. They are not waiting for God. They are searching for their own truths. There is a group and I don't like them. There is a group that wants to de-stabilize the United States and break down its unity, but the grace of God is greater than anything, and the Holy Spirit is exerting His graces. The Holy Spirit is pouring His graces abundantly."

You will find more on her prophecies both in the body of this book and in the new, extensive, updated epilogue. For now we must know the urgency of praying the twenty decades of the Rosary each day (including the new Luminous Mysteries); of praying with the family; and of praying for the world. That's what Maria and her loved ones do. We've never seen a family like it, and here you see the real fruit. Love. Devotion.

No one likes to be away from Maria once they have been around her. She leaves a terrific sense of joy, and so far there is no one we have seen quite like her. As you will note in the following pages, Maria's cheer — her joy in Christ, the Blessed Mother, and the company of angels — continues to the present, although she believes we will see more trials and another earth-shaking event. The world is entering a "new stage," she says, and in many ways, this is good; there will be greater light from heaven. She sees this enlightenment beginning around 2004. What that could be is anyone's guess. It is noteworthy that not long after Maria mentioned 2004, there was word that the Pope was declaring 2004 a year of special Eucharistic devotion. He even mentioned "rivers of light" — which Maria had also mentioned!

And so, despite everything, we head into the future with optimism and we note her demeanor of calmness, prayerfulness, and vigilance. According to Maria, we are entering a time that will see disturbances in nature. She has long seen a build-up in such events, smaller ones that will precipitate into ones that are much larger, until there is a reawakening. She has warned that the earth's core "is not in balance" and when asked about earthquakes (while visiting the New York area) said, "I feel one close to this place, this area. And a lot of water is involved — close to this area. *But we can stop all that with prayer.* With prayer from our hearts this may be stopped. Prayer is the fundamental base in order to help mankind. We must be alert to save our souls and deserve what God has planned for us. I leave these things in the Hands of the Lord. He knows. He knows what He is doing. I know my condition is delicate, but I will do my best until the last moment. That's what the Lord wants us to do."

Maria has expressed special concern for the safety of children. In 2001, at the height of anxiety over terrorist attacks, she released a specific message about this. "Watch out for the children," she said, a veiled utterance which she did not elaborate upon. We posted this warning on our website (to pray for children) and like many others worried that terrorists were ready to strike at schools or get at our youngest in other ways. Now we're wondering if Maria was referring instead to what we are seeing unfold before our eyes: the incredible saga of child abductions. Since Maria issued her warning, there have been famous cases in California, Utah, Texas, and Pennsylvania. Moreover, the D.C. sniper specifically threatened our young. Maria has also warned that immediately going to war over terrorist incidents is "a mistake" because it would set many negatives in motion. "The U.S. is smart and should wait patiently," she advised. Instead of war, she urges the United States to turn to prayer, meditation, penance, and the Eucharist, what she calls the four "pillars." She believes if this happens, the U.S. will be unharmed, in the long run, by disasters.

It's not the fight against terrorism that concerns her but that the U.S. may fall (and by this reading may already have fallen) into a "provocation." "Definitely it's going to escalate but at the same time through prayer we can stop a big thing from happening," she said in 2001, adding that the attacks in New York City and at the Pentagon were allowed by God as "an awakening of conscience" to strengthen the U.S. spiritually, along with the rest of the world. "I know the wound has been very big, but now we have to see the situation through God's eyes and ask for forgiveness, for courage, and for the will to pray and do penance and rid ourselves of pride," she intoned.

"Our Lord is crying out at us for conversions," added the seer. "This has been a lesson for the whole world. The faith of people in today's world is too superficial. We must have a heart opened to the Lord and His grace, because God is now going to shake the whole world, not only the U.S. It will not be a violent shaking but something that makes people aware of His Presence."

As you will see in the epilogue, such a purification was to occur late in 2002 at Betania itself.

You will see further prophecies too. "Even though times look so bad, it is glorious," says Maria. "We are going through glorious times. It will make everything better. Many signs are being disclosed. We should be only joyful. Everything is in God's control."

In the pages that follow (remember, the initial interviews were conducted in the late 1980s and early 1990s) you will also see what amounts to a prophecy of the current Church crisis — the scandal of abuse. "This Church is holy, immaculate, perfect," she had said long ago, "but the men in it can be imperfect, sinners, with weaknesses." As you will see, those interviews are followed by ones conducted in 2002 and 2003 (in the epilogue).

The important point: we must know what to pray about. Right now is a prophetic time — and prophecy is foremost. *At the same time we must have balance and we must not obsess on the negative*. Could it be that after all the struggles a great day of light will come? Using words similar to those recently employed by the Pope, Maria speaks about the arrival of a "new earth" that will begin with an increase in God's grace (a heightening of our awareness) as God radiates His special light from heaven.

"I feel that here on earth, we will have beautiful things in the future that will resemble, will reflect, the things of heaven," says Maria. "Here on earth we are going to see beautiful cities that are going to be built in a resemblance of heaven, like the coming of God's kingdom — a new world. There will be like communities all over the world. We will live in communities. We are already beginning trials, a time of trials, and these trials will come to help people realize the importance of helping each other. People will realize that without their brothers, they cannot go on. It will start from the year 2004 on. It will be the beginning. Rivers of supernatural light are awaiting us — surprises, beautiful surprises. Each one of us will encounter ourselves, and beautiful ideas will come to our minds, beautiful talents, and more than anything else, we will achieve the simplicity of innocent children. And that's the most important thing. We will be able to achieve the innocence of a child but with the maturity and knowledge, the wisdom, of an adult."

"It has to be that way, because otherwise God can not enter our souls and hearts," continues Maria. "When this light arrives it comes with supernatural light and God will allow us to feel His Presence deep in our hearts — the divine spark that will awaken our conscience, to help us realize that God is everything and we are nothing without Him. When we get this light we will be able to feel God in our hearts again. We will feel Him all the time with us."

"*My children, I am with you day and night,*" she says she was told by Jesus. "*I live among you. And I will give you My light.*"

"With this votive light, this continuous light, will come hope, strength, and the will to be able to do things in the right way," adds Maria. "We must try to live each day with His presence on our minds and hearts. If your brother wants to live in a different way, just let him walk his path. Never try to force. We must try to show the harmony and love of God in our behavior."

She has borne special concern for Israel. Normally upbeat, the seer warns that events in the Middle East have escalated to the point where they could now trigger a world war. "She is so sad about what is going on in Israel," says her son-in-law Carlos. "Her face is like the face of the Lord. You can't imagine how she felt when she heard of a statue of the Blessed Virgin that was damaged in Bethlehem [by gunfire]. She is saying that they are using their free will in the wrong way. They must stop because it can get out of control. They are creating a monster. It will never end. They must put an end to this as soon as possible. She is praying to prevent that war and expects a miracle to stop it."

While the mystic has long indicated dangers in the Middle East, it is unusual for Esperanza to issue such a stark warning. Although she has often mentioned dangers brewing in both the Orient and the Middle East, she had not previously warned of a full-scale international conflict. Carlos quoted her as saying that "many see it as a battle of 'good' versus 'evil,' but it is not for us to declare who is good or bad. God loves everyone, and so we must look and pray for a resolution."

In addition to Parkinson's, Maria still receives stigmata on Good Fridays — although it is no longer visible. On Good Friday, 2002, she experienced the pains of crucifixion in her hands, feet, and on her shoulder. Carlos reports that the famous mystic made the Stations of the Cross holding a cross in a wheelchair. She and her family confirm that she still has daily visions, which, as you will see in the following introduction, began in 1933, when she was only five. Asked if she could tell if others were seeing Jesus or the Virgin Mary, Esperanza said that she could, and smiled when asked if she thought the Pope has had visions.

Although she has mentioned 2004 as a year of special grace, *she presents no specific frame of time* for events in the larger picture. She says that after such events, after tribulation, there will be a renewal and that whenever it comes, this renewal will be both physical and spiritual. There will be a new time; she sees events leading to a "light"; and that, she says, will pave the way to what she mysteriously describes as "a new dawn of Jesus." In the epilogue, she discusses more about what she sees as a major coming manifestation of Jesus.

This is a remarkable woman and in realizing her effect on people, I recall the account of a man who had been chef to the rich and famous (from Frank Sinatra to Princess Di). This man had a restaurant with photos of many celebrities. Then he met Maria — whom he had not even heard of before — and soon her photograph took center stage in his place, above all others. I first met Maria Esperanza in 1992 and I'll never forget the experience. She was at a hospital in Caracas at the time — her daughter was having a child — but she was gracious enough to come into a nearby waiting room. Later we met at her house. Through the years we have kept in touch. She is a good friend — as well as one incredible mystic.

PART I

Esperanza

CHAPTER 1

Rose of Love

Since 1981, when the Virgin Mary was first reported in Medjugorje, Yugoslavia, there has been a veritable explosion of private revelations. Each week we hear of a new locutionist or seer. It's gotten to the point where just about each diocese has its own visionary.

They've shown up everywhere from CNN to the news magazines. There are locutionists who have special medals struck. There are "visionaries" who hold court at apparition sites or write down messages from Jesus.

I have no idea how many of these folks are true and how many are the products of an overactive subconscious. I fear the number of false seers is significant. Surely some are victims of delusion, diabolical deception, or wishful thinking. I've met as many as four or five seers while staying overnight in a single American city.

As I said, I don't know how many are deceptions and how many are part of a great outpouring of the Holy Spirit in our special times. I know only this: If there is one seer who distinguishes herself in this great chaos—in the eruption of mysticism that is sweeping from Europe to the Americas, and even into Africa—it is the matronly woman who is the subject of this book.

Her name is Maria Esperanza Medrano de Bianchini

and she lives on the hillsides of Caracas, Venezuela.

You are about to encounter her in an extraordinary series of interviews.

She is a seer, yes; she has experienced apparitions now for sixty years. But she is also a stigmatist, a prophet, and a healer. Indeed, some of the most unforgettable charisms associated with historical saints are reported around Maria. There are those who have themselves witnessed the Virgin in Maria's company, while others have watched as a Host miraculously appears in her mouth or have seen strange clouds and luminosities.

Like some of the more remarkable saints, Esperanza has also been seen to levitate in ecstasy and appear in bilocation. Or so they claim. When Maria is experiencing her visions, a remarkable blue butterfly often flits from a Lourdes grotto at the apparition site of Betania, where observers also note the sound of an invisible choir or the strong scent of roses—so strong it has been compared to a bottle of spilt perfume.

The bishop himself has witnessed phenomena, and so respected is Maria that she is allowed to have the Blessed Sacrament in her own home.

Priests, nuns, and bishops seek her spiritual counsel.

So let me get right to the point: The interviews you are about to read are with a woman who not only stands above the clutter of seers, but a woman who, if just half of what they say is true, is one of the major mystics of this century.

There is always a big "if." I am not qualified to judge Maria's authenticity. I make no such conclusion. I know only that those closest to her testify to her love and devotion. Her name is Maria Esperanza de Bianchini but they call her "Esperanza," which means "hope." Her central message is that salvation is best worked out by practicing Christian love and reconciliation. I use the word "extraordinary" to describe Maria because, with the exception of the seers in Medjugorje, no modern mystics have left as deep and lasting an impression on pilgrims. She's not your standard "visionary." Nor, as far as I can tell, are her phenomena the product of hysteria, exaggeration, or imagination. While Maria herself is not officially sanctioned by the Church (virtually no living mystic ever is), the apparition site of Betania *has* been formally approved—perhaps the firmest Church approval since Beauraing or Fatima—and word of Maria's personal charisms have reached the ears of several popes and Padre Pio.

Indeed, for a while Padre Pio served as Maria's spiritual director. He had mentioned to friends that he would soon be visited by an extraordinary woman. "There is a young woman who is going to come from South America," Pio told one of his spiritual daughters. "When I leave, she will be your consolation."

The incredible old priest heard of Maria before she first visited, and once, when Maria and her husband journeyed, as often she did, to Pio's church in San Giovanni Rotundo, he saw her and exclaimed, "Ah, Esperanza!"

Or so goes the story. Whatever the accuracy of particular details—which are often hard to corroborate due to various circumstances such as the language barrier—Maria Esperanza seems to be a woman of destiny. She's a seer who has experienced apparitions since the age of five. She's a stigmatist who under the close observance of doctors has suffered the bleeding wounds of Christ on Good Fridays. She's a prophet who brings both hope and warning to a tumultuous and increasingly evil world.

Esperanza! Her name comes as an exclamation. Her presence comes with the glow of joy. She is a living and breathing font of the Spirit, a wife, mother, grandmother, and friend.

She is a gatherer of souls for the Blessed Virgin.

That is what so many who have had a personal audience with her (as opposed to watching from afar) seem to claim. Many visitors are startled by Maria's ability to "read" souls, and indeed when I first met Maria she told me things about myself that she could not possibly have known. I realize such knowledge can also come from occult sources, but what I found most impressive was the feeling of love—unconditional and joyful love—that pours forth from Maria. There is a remarkable cognizance—as well as an unforgettable twinkle—in her scrutinizing brown eyes. Despite her incredible spiritual life she is able to maintain a solid household and delights in baking for and serving her many visitors. Everyone who has spent time around Esperanza and her radiant family seems to have benefitted from their extraordinary spirituality.

These are the first "fruits" we look for in a visionary. We don't judge them solely on clever or dramatic messages, nor simply upon the phenomena, which can be a counterfeit by demons. We don't declare an apparition divine just because the sun spins or miraculous images appear in a photograph. We evaluate a seer's personality and family life. We look for *personal* fruits. We look for love, devotion, and humility.

The local bishop believes that Maria passes those tests, and when it does come to phenomena, no current visionary, not even in Medjugorje, has encountered a wider array of reportedly paranormal experiences.

Those phenomena are attested to not only by the many pilgrims who seek out Esperanza but also by nuns, priests, bishops, theologians, businessmen, ranking medical doctors, engineers, psychologists, and even an army general.

Though no one would claim she is his equal, observers have compared Esperanza to Pio himself.

As you will see in her own words, Esperanza and the apparition site of Betania seem to serve as an experience of God's Mercy. In Medjugorje, where the Virgin has been appearing since 1981, I found the special charism of peace. At Fatima I found the charism of knowledge. At Betania—which, like Fatima, has been sanctioned by the Church—I found the charism of joy.

Those who are around Maria often find themselves musically inspired even if they are not normally so inclined. A beautiful choir has been organized at Betania, and the bishop himself was so moved that he wrote a song about Betania.

The interviews that follow were conducted by Drew J. Mariani, a young and exceptional film producer from Lima, Pennsylvania. Mariani's work is well-known to those in the Marian Movement. His bestselling video *Marian Apparitions of the Twentieth Century* remains a seminal work on the Virgin's warnings to mankind, and his recent video on the events in Venezuela, *Betania—Land of Grace* (available through Marian Communications, Box 8, Lima, Pennsylvania, 19037), has similarly found its quick place in the annals of Mariology.

The interviews, conducted from 1989 to 1993, have been edited for general consumption and most of the questions have been framed and interposed to facilitate the reader's understanding of what Maria and her witnesses are saying. In other words, I have used the literary device of inserting questions created after the interviews for clarification, and any opinions expressed in them are my own. I also have injected portions of my own conversations with Esperanza, and I brushed up the construction and translation, using composite quotes on occasion but quotes which are nonetheless true to the interviews.

It is largely through Mariani's efforts that Esperanza's story has surfaced, garnering the attention of Catholics and even non-Catholics throughout North America. It's a story that I hope you find to be an inspiration. Virtually every aspect of Esperanza's life has possessed mystical components. Even her birth, on November 22, 1928, is of interest. Her mother had desperately wanted a daughter—she already had three boys—and asked the Blessed Virgin, who through history had appeared at many South American locations, especially in Venezuela—to grant her a girl.

True to a prophecy, Maria was born in Barrancas on the feast day of Saint Cecilia, who is associated with music. The birth occurred while Maria's mother was taking a trip by boat and in fact arriving at a port in search of better medical facilities. It was a very painful delivery, and during her pregnancy Maria's mother had often prayed before a picture of the Blessed Mother—offering the child to Mary and promising to name the child Maria (Spanish for Mary) and Esperanza (as I said, the Spanish word for "hope") if it was a girl.

So came into the world "Mary Hope," destined to shine like a star, destined to be a great instrument of the Holy Spirit. She was a sick, suffering child who recovered from mysterious disorders in a miraculous way. Like all that is worthwhile, she was prepared and purified through suffering, surviving severe heart and respiratory maladies. As a child Maria showed a precocious interest in religious matters, often playing with dolls that were dressed as priests and nuns. At the age of five, while bidding her mother, who was taking a trip, farewell at the port of Bolivar City, Maria saw a smiling woman rise from the Orinoco River with a rose in her hand.

It was an apparition, she knows now, of Saint Thèrése of Lisieux, the "Little Flower."

The rose Saint Thèrése held was extraordinarily beautiful, a brilliant red flower that she threw to young Maria.

Her mother immediately proclaimed the rose a sign of God's endearment.

Such claimed phenomena are difficult even for the seasoned believer to comprehend. It is only after spending a while with Esperanza that one begins to integrate the realism and pattern of her experiences. In later years many around her were to witness other phenomena related to roses, including the inexplicable falling of rose petals at Betania and in Maria's own home. When I visited her in 1991, I was told that just a few days earlier, petals had appeared on the stairs leading up to the second floor. I smelled the sudden scent of roses in Maria's living room.

Such alleged phenomena are regular happenings around Esperanza. So are the "coincidences." Feast days of the saints, especially those of Mary, figure prominently into Esperanza's diary. She received First Communion on July 16, 1937, the feast day of Our Lady of Carmen, and soon after the young Esperanza encountered tremendous physiological tribulation. By the age of 12 she had developed such an acute case of pneumonia that her doctor didn't think she would live more than three days.

"Mother of mine, would it be that you want me to come to you?" Maria asked.

She then prayed, waiting for an answer.

When she opened her eyes, the Blessed Virgin was smiling in front of her.

Our Lady appeared to Maria as the Virgin of the Valley of Margarita (another apparition site off the coast of Venezuela) and told the girl what medication to take. Maria later learned that her father had a special devotion to the Virgin of the Valley, and on his deathbed he had called upon the Virgin to protect his wife and children. Our Lady's remedy turned out to be the medication that cured Maria.

There were other trials during her youth, and so sick was Maria that she was fed through injection. Still, the young Esperanza never wavered in her faith. Praying another time for Christ to take her so she would no longer be such a burden to her family, Maria opened her eyes and this time saw the Heart of Jesus.

It was full of light and dripping blood.

"He was strong," recalls Maria. "His eyes, how they penetrate. It's like radar (the way) He penetrates you with His eyes! It was so beautiful, beautiful eyes. . . His face was so gentle."

When He appeared to Maria, Christ addressed her as *"My white rose of love."*

Instead of granting her death, the Lord and His Mother came to heal her. But they explained that life is a long series of trials, and that the bridge to Heaven is constructed through trials, purgation, and humility—especially humility. *"My daughter, when you begin your pilgrimage you will have many sufferings,"* Our Lady told her. *"They are the pain of this mother. Help me. Help me to save this lost world."*

So began Maria's journey. So began her life of mysticism. Her marriage was typically providential. At first she wanted to become a nun and entered a convent in 1954. That same year, on October 3, at the end of a Mass, she had yet another implausible experience. Once again, Saint Thèrése of the Child Jesus appeared to her, and once more a rose was thrown to her. But this time when Maria went to catch it, as she had done as a girl of five, it wasn't a rose that landed in her hand. Rather, something pinched her right palm and blood began to seep from that hand. It was the onset of the stigmata. *"This is not your vocation, yours is to be a wife and mother,"* the Little Flower instructed her. Maria felt at that moment that she would eventually leave the convent and become a mother, working for the Lord in the world. Her vocation was to be that of a family woman.

Soon after, Maria, still unsure of her future course, went to Rome to live at the Ravasco Institute, run by Daughters of the Hearts of Jesus and Mary at the Vatican. On August 22, 1954, back in Caracas, she was instructed about Betania and the blue butterfly.

One day Esperanza saw the apparition of a man waving a flag that was white, red, and green, a sign that her future husband would be an Italian. An apparition of John Bosco announced to her that she would meet her future husband on November 1, 1955. On October 12, the feast of the Virgin of Pilar, she had another experience with Mary, and the following year she returned to Rome, where, in front of the Church of the Sacred Heart of Jesus, she met Geo Bianchini Gianni on November 1, as was foretold to her.

An irresistible power overtook Geo and he pursued Maria even though Esperanza was living with nuns.

The following October 13, anniversary of the great Fatima miracle, Our Blessed Mother told Maria she would be married on December 8, 1956—yet another feast day, this time the feast of the Immaculate Conception. Geo and Maria were indeed married that day in the choir chapel of the Immaculate Conception at St. Peter's Basilica. No one had ever been married there during Advent, and it was only after a cleric, Monsignor Julio Rossi, parish priest at St. Peter's, noticed the incredible aura around Maria, as well as the scent of roses, that he went to Pope Pius XII, who knew of Maria and secured final approval for a marriage ceremony in the historical chapel.

December 8 was also Geo's birthday.

Their first child, a daughter, was named Maria Inmaculada.

Thus we see the hand of God at every turn. Thus we see how God works, when we beseech Him. Nothing was more fateful than the visit from a friend who came to ask for help during a drought. The cattle on his land were stricken with hunger and Maria told Geo they should go see the land. When they did, in March of 1974, they immediately fell in love with the picturesque hillside located about an hour and a half from Caracas. It was the fulfillment of yet another prophecy. For many years Maria and Geo had been on the lookout for the land which the Virgin had shown her as a young woman. It was to be a special land with an old house, a waterfall, and a grotto. Maria had even discussed the vision with Padre Pio.

Now they had found it. It was a hillside known as Finca Betania.

"From 1957 until 1974, we searched for this land in all of Venezuela," Geo explains. "In 1974, in February, we heard about a farm and decided, 'Let's see it.' We called the guy in March and went to see it. When we arrived, Maria said, 'We have to buy this farm.' In June we signed the contract. We purchased the land with Jesus Andrew, an engineer, and Jose Castellano, an attorney. We were glad to do this, as we had dreamt of this for many years.

It corresponded exactly with a vision my wife had been given when she was a very young girl."

Betania is situated amidst aluminum shanties, banana farms, and tropical mountains, about 12 miles from the village of Cua. It is a region of the river called Tuy, which ironically, or perhaps providentially, is the same name as the town in Spain where Sister Lucia dos Santos of Fatima experienced visions in a convent. There was an old sugar mill on the land, and although it wasn't apparent at first, a stream and waterfall were also located on the property. As time elapsed they placed a statue of Our Lady of Lourdes, also known as the Virgin of the Immaculate Conception.

Geo and his partners purchased the land and cleared the hillside. The clearing became their sanctuary. They grew accustomed to visiting the farm on Saturdays, praying and taking care of the livestock. In February of 1976, while Maria was in Italy tending to Geo's ailing mother, the Virgin told Esperanza to head back for Venezuela and prepare herself for something that was to happen at Betania on March 25, 1976. *"You shall see me on the land your purchased,"* the Virgin announced simply and unforgettably.

Maria did as she was told, arriving at Betania on March 25—feast of the Annunciation. They were reciting the Rosary when suddenly Our Blessed Mother appeared, calling herself "Mary, Reconciler of Peoples and Nations."

"My heart I gave to you. My heart I give to you. My heart I will always give to you."

It was the onset of apparitions that continue at Betania to this day. I should emphasize that while they intertwine, the apparition site is independent of Esperanza. Events take place at Betania with or without Maria. The most momentous of these occurred on March 25, 1984, when seven successive apparitions were witnessed by a total of 108 people. It was this event that started Bishop

Pio Bello Ricardo's investigation.

In the days and months that followed, hundreds and then thousands saw the Mother of God at Betania. She appeared as the Virgin of the Miraculous Medal, grace streaming from her downward palms, or as the exquisite Virgin of Lourdes. In the following pages you'll see descriptions from the witnesses. Bishop Pio Bello personally interviewed several hundred of these witnesses and took about 550 written statements (some with more than one signature, such that at least a thousand people actually signed their names to the documents). He then traveled to Rome and confided the incredible happenings to Joseph Cardinal Ratzinger, cardinal prefect of the Sacred Congregation for the Doctrine of the Faith, and to the Pope himself.

With reports of miraculous, supernatural, or extraordinary events within a diocese, it is the local bishop's authority to approve or denounce the claimed events, and Rome only intervenes if it disagrees with the bishop's assessment or disapproves of his manner of investigation. No such disapproval was forthcoming from the Vatican, and after meditating on his decision for three years, Bishop Pio Bello issued a pastoral letter declaring that the Betania apparitions not only conform with Scripture and Church teachings but also "are authentic, they are supernatural, and they are of a divine source." According to Pio Bello, 35 of Venezuela's 37 bishops and auxiliary bishops allowed his assessment.

As a journalist my attention was sparked by the bishop's unusually strong and indeed fervent approval. I realize a bishop is human and can be wrong. But what can we do but follow the leaders of the Church? And what can we do but observe with our own eyes? I myself witnessed extraordinary manifestations in December of 1991, while praying at the site of apparitions. The solar phenomena were even more spectacular than what I had witnessed during several trips to Medjugorje. Suddenly, a shaft of light radiated from the sun and formed a detailed and perfect image of Our Lady of the Miraculous Medal.

It was a manifestation of Mary from the waist up, and a moment later it drew back up into the sun.

The testimonies of others could fill a large volume. One observer, Dr. Vinicio Arrieta, former director of a school of medicine, estimates that more than 10,000 people have seen the Virgin at Betania. They most commonly see her as a type of living marble statue or as a manifestation formed in luminous light, smoke, or clouds.

Pilgrims also see a "glitter" or sparkly radiance that falls from the sky and strange lights in the heavens. A giant cross has also appeared above the mountain, and there have been many cures. According to Dr. Arrieta, who studied at Harvard, there have been more than 1,000 physical healings at Betania. He himself was cured of prostate cancer that had metastazied to his spine. Others have been cured of paralysis, liver disorders, and leukemia.

According to scientist Samir Gebran, a doctor of immunology and Maria's son-in-law, strange relics have been found at Betania. He says that on December 14, 1985, Maria Esperanza felt compelled to go to the creek, where she spotted a rock, pulled it from the creekbed, and in turning it over saw that it held a white image of the Virgin.

Immediately those around her could detect the scent of roses.

"After the Rosary she opened her hands," says Gebran. "She was close to the altar and rose petals appeared on her hands."

Another son-in-law, Juan Carlos, told me how as a newlywed staying with Esperanza he would pad downstairs in the middle of the night and see Maria in the chapel, deep in prayer and surrounded by a large halo.

Still others have seen her feet rise several inches off the floor during Consecration at Mass or have encountered unearthly, luminous fogs.

Another of Esperanza's daughters, Maria Gracia, claims that on March 25, 1977, it seemed like Betania was on fire. "When we looked up, the cloud opened up and a light came out," she says. "Well, it just blinded me. And I went to my knees and I felt this force push me. I tried to look, but I couldn't. And then I saw my mother was looking, was looking up so peacefully. And she looked so beautiful. Tears were coming down her cheeks. And in that moment she had the phenomenon of levitation. It was just beautiful."

Most incredible are the claims, again made by competent observers, that on 14 occasions a stemmed rose has pushed out from the skin near Maria's bosom. The rose witnessed was an actual flower, red and touched with dew. This, of course, is nearly impossible to believe, and although similar phenomena have been associated with at least one past saint, I maintain both an open mind and skepticism. But many are those—including, again, unusually competent observers—who claim to have *seen* it happen before their incredulous eyes. A rose coming out of Maria's bosom! It is a phenomenon that causes Esperanza great pain and at the same time a phenomenon that provokes joy and love—once more, the fruit of holy suffering.

What are we to make of such accounts? Is Maria Esperanza a modern, female version of Padre Pio? Or is it all too much to believe?

Let me repeat that we must be careful. Even the most

well-intentioned can be deceived. Maria Esperanza would be the first to admit that she is not infallible. How could I, or anyone else, ever say that there won't be doubts and controversies? There will be. Maria is a human with human faults. Her words are not all etched in granite. A number of things she says are her own personal opinions or prognostications. Not every word comes from the heavenlies!

As with any reputed visionary, a personal element can be injected into a mystical experience, thus distorting that experience. In other cases her predictions have been mistakenly reported. For instance, in April of 1993 she said there would be "movements in the direction of peace" in Bosnia within three months, but that if there was not enough prayer, obstacles would remain. According to her interpreter, Kathy Chebly, this was mistakenly reported as a flat prediction of the war's end—which of course did not come. There have been several such instances of miscommunication.

Still, I respect the caution and skepticism. There is nothing more difficult to judge than mysticism. I would never make a final conclusion myself. I have seen too many men of more experience than I—well-known theologians—stumble into highly deceptive apparitions. As a journalist I cannot rule out the same possibility here. And so I maintain a cautious optimism. We must remember that there are always "gray" areas with mystics, and that an open vessel for the Spirit can also occasionally be a vessel for subconscious forces.

Let me repeat: I am personally very impressed with Maria, and especially the true love and devotion shown by her children (who, even if it means traveling many miles, yearn to be by her side), but like the Church I must wait to see how everything runs its course. There are certain questions that need to be addressed. A number of observers are perplexed by Maria's tendency to lapse into a semi-trance and speak in the Virgin's voice. For some, this phenomenon is a bit too close to spirit channeling.

From what I can tell there is a difference between what Maria does and the New Age channeling rampant in America. Maria's is more a case of what is known in mystical theology as "holy possession," whereby, like the Apostles (*Acts* 2:2-4), a mystic is filled with the Holy Spirit. It signifies complete surrender to God. So does her stigmata, which developed into open wounds in 1967, after years of invisible stigmata (only the pains of such wounds). I believe Maria is an extremely gifted and holy person, although, as a journalist, I must always maintain my guard.

However true and good a visionary seems at first, we must always maintain our vigilance. The New Age is infiltrating everywhere. I implore you with all sincerity: *pray fervently to the Holy Spirit before you read about any mystics. Spend a hundred times as many hours reading Scripture, attending Mass, and praying the Rosary as you do reading, hearing about, or visiting visionaries.*

This goes for Medjugorje, and it also goes for Maria.

But I do believe there is something extraordinary going on at Betania, something that seems to be extraordinarily good. We should never idolize a mystic, and we should remember that it is Betania that the Church has approved, not any specific seer. However, we should also respect those who are true to their call, and Maria is as true as any with whom I am familiar. Her presence is intense. It is as though she travels between dimensions. So far, from all that I can tell, she is a major force of goodness and perhaps the most unusual person I have met in my many years of journalism.

If Esperanza has missed a prophecy on occasion, she is in the company of other mystics, including Saint Catherine of Laboure, who have now and then been off the mark with their forecasts. More importantly, Esperanza hits a bullseye when it comes to most attributes of personality. There is cohesion in her persona. There is also great cohesion in her family. And whether or not onlookers misinterpret certain cultural or mystical traits, the Maria I met was a woman of profound caring, intelligence, and humility. She is full of love.

Although, like any mystic, her phenomena are not sanctioned by the Church, they have as yet met no ecclesiastical condemnation. And meanwhile, the site with which she is associated, namely Betania, has been about as "approved" as a site can be.

"It seems to me that Maria Bianchini is a very, very good person, a very good Christian," says Bishop Pio Bello, whose diocese includes Betania. "She has a great prayerful spirit. I would like for my own self the spirit of prayer that she has and the union with God that she has and her constant contact with God. For her there is nothing strange about her spending a whole night in prayer, all night in long prayer."

The peculiar way in which Maria transmits information didn't seem to put off the bishop, whose pastoral letter of November 21, 1987, is partly reproduced in the appendix to this book. As I said, it was one of the strongest endorsements of an apparition this century. Bishop Pio wasn't just saying that the messages are in accordance with Scripture and Church teaching; he was declaring them directly authentic and declaring Betania to be "sacred" ground. As a psychologist and professor of spirituality, the bishop was more than qualified to investigate the matter, and the fact that he personally interviewed the witnesses, as well as consulted with

Pope John Paul II and Joseph Cardinal Ratzinger while weighing his discernment, lends all the more weight to his final decision. While the Vatican itself usually makes no formal pronouncements on such issues, preferring to leave it in the hands of the local ordinary, its quiet assent signaled approval of the bishop's pastoral letter. Indeed, the Pope told Bishop Pio that the proliferation of such apparitions appears to be a "sign of the times" (see *Matthew* 16:3).

The Virgin comes as "Mary, Virgin and Mother Reconciler of People and Nations" to sow brotherhood on a cold and egotistical planet. Mankind, she warns, is *"moving toward perdition. If there is no change or improvement of life, you will succumb under fire: war and death. We want to halt the evil that suffocates you. We want to overcome the spirit of rebellion and the darkness of oppression by the enemy. This is why, again, in this century, my Divine Son arises . . ."*

Maria was told by the Virgin that this is the *"hour of decision for humanity."* The world will face a *"very serious moment"* soon. There is the danger of massive war, especially in Asia and the former republics of the Soviet Union, and she warns about a potential atomic catastrophe as well as natural calamities. We face plagues like those of ancient Egypt, all because humankind, in it intellectual arrogance, has turned toward materialism and away from God. It is Maria's opinion that the period 1992 to 1995 has and will serve as the very beginning of God's "justice in the world." Indeed, we have already seen the onset of this justice in the strange occurrences afflicting many parts of the world—the earth tremors shaking Japan, the blizzards, hurricanes, and droughts, the flooding along the Mississippi. During the summer of 1993 a devastating storm hit the region of Betania itself and so too have we seen a red flag of warning in the terrible conflict surrounding Medjugorje in Bosnia-Hercegovina.

These are just the beginning: little clues or "pre-signs." In many ways the same is indicated at Medjugorje, where the Virgin mentioned twice during 1993 that we need to discern the *"signs of the times."* According to Mary of Medjugorje, and now Betania, we are in a *"special time"* during which Heaven is trying to draw us out of a great and oppressing darkness; a time of great evil.

But with those serious warnings, warnings that we ignore at our own peril, comes great hope. With simplicity, humility, and brotherly love, we can defeat darkness and mitigate potential disasters. Most importantly, with love we can help win souls for Heaven. Maria has been granted visions concerning a future manifestation of Christ—a manifestation in which Christ will show Himself in a powerful way. Maria told me on September 18, 1993, that some kind of event will occur in the not-too-distant future that everyone will notice. I couldn't discern if this mega-event, or whatever it might be, will be pleasant or painful.

This manifestation will mark the end of the great darkness that has bedimmed our spiritual intelligence and obscured our century.

"A great moment is approaching," the Virgin told Esperanza. *"A great day of light!"*

As you will notice, Esperanza does not foresee the end of the world. She sees a coming purification. Difficult times will arrive, but in the end, says Esperanza, it will make us better people. The world will improve. It will solve many of its problems. It will draw closer to Heaven.

"Jesus will have a great surprise. We will see Him in

glory with rays of light. The last messages are beautiful —it's incredible the way He will come in glory."

And so is Betania itself a sign of the times, a sign of Divine Love, a sign of charity—a sign that after the current tribulations, there will be a new and better world.

It is a sign that the afterlife does exist, that God is watching, that there really is Heaven.

And it's a sign that love and humility—especially love—form the bridge to Heaven.

Michael H. Brown
Latham, N.Y. September 29, 1993

CHAPTER 2

Early Years: The Flame of Jesus

Maria, tell us a bit about your life. What were the circumstances of your birth?

Before I was born, my mother and my father had three boys, three sons. And my mother spent five years without having another child, and she waited for a daughter. She asked the Blessed Mother of Carmen to give her a daughter, a young girl, a young girl to be the joy of her heart. My godmother, the lady who became my godmother afterwards, went before a statue of Jesus, Jesus of Good Hope, and said to the statue, "Jesus of Good Hope, help [Maria's mother]. Help her bring her daughter into the world happy, that if it's a boy it will be called 'Jesus,' and if it's a girl it will be called 'Maria.' " The day I was born was November 22, 1928, the day of Saint Cecilia, who was associated with music and singing. It was a very strange birth. My mother suffered very much. But she thanked God because I was all right, everything was all right. I had a very happy childhood. It was just wonderful.

At the age of five your mother had to leave town for a while and you saw her off at the port. That was when Saint Thérése the Little Flower first appeared to you. Can you tell us a bit more about that dramatic episode?

My mother was going to travel, and it happened that that day my mother was going to leave—we were at the port to say good-bye to her. My little sister, who was younger than I, began to scream and cry. For me it was a little strange, but I didn't [scream or cry]. We could say that I was a little separated, a distance from this. I would play with my dolls, who were priests and nuns. All my dolls were religious people. When we were at the port saying good-bye to my mother, I was on the dock and everyone was saying good-bye to my mother, and I stared at the river that was coming very strongly at us. I was watching waves that were really strong and were going up and down. And I remained there, staring. I had a pain in my heart, feeling as if I couldn't separate myself from my mother. When I saw Saint Thèrése. . . it seems like a distant dream right now. I saw Saint Thèrése smiling with these big beautiful blue eyes. How precious. And she stayed there staring at me.

Many visionaries see Jesus, Mary, or other heavenly visitors in different ways. The Virgin often comes in different appearances according to the culture and circumstances. We realize that heavenly entities can make themselves appear any way they want to. For example, Saint Thèrése had brown eyes, yet you saw them differently.

There was such a blue, an intense blue in her eyes, almost green. It was such an intense color, it tore at my heart. And she smiled. She arose from the waters, came from the waters and smiled at me. I'm trying to recall everything now, when I was there looking, watching Saint Thèrése coming up from the water with a rose in her hand. It was a very, very beautiful red rose. And she threw it at me. And I moved around. I don't know how I did it, but I caught it in my hands. And I was so little at the time. I was playing, and I ran to my mother who was leaving, and we were all saying good-bye to her. And I said, "Mom, Saint Thèrése, Saint Thèrése." And my mother said to me, "Oh, my love, God gave you this rose."

And Saint Thèrése continued to be important through your childhood?

At eight years old I made my First Communion, the day of the Virgin of Carmen, July 16. It was a very beautiful day for me and for my soul. It was like the greatest gift which the Lord could have given me, to receive Him in my heart. I asked Saint Thèrése to teach me to feel her presence. I was playing, but I felt her presence. I would tell her about my little things, my desires, my wants. And especially I would talk to her of a hospital where everyone who had nowhere to go could go and be well taken care of, with good doctors, with good nurses. And one day I really felt that she told me that this day would arrive, and I am still waiting for it.

As a child you were very sickly, especially as you approached your teen years.

I became asthmatic. I had difficulty breathing. Bronchial pneumonia overcame me. The doctors said it was acute pneumonia. I was so seriously ill that the doctor told my mother, "I don't think she'll live more than three days because it is in her lungs, and everything is serious—her heart has weakened."

One afternoon, probably 4:30 or 5:00 or something like that, I told my Holy Mother, "Mother of mine, would it be that you want me to come to you? Because maybe Saint Thèrése wants to take me to her side." I closed my eyes as if I was waiting for an answer, and when I opened my eyes I found myself in front of her. She was in front of me smiling. It was Our Lady of the Valley of Margarita.

You recovered at that time, thanks to the Virgin, and then had a relapse?

Another serious moment arrived. I was still so young. I would have been about 14 or 15 years old, and it was so painful. It was my heart. My heart was weakening. I had a heart condition, about 150 beats a minute, which would make me faint, and they would have to take me to the hospital, where they gave me treatments. I couldn't breathe. It was an incredible agony.

The problems continued through your teen years?

On November 8 in 1947, that was when I really got bad. I couldn't get up for three months. The doctors didn't know what to do. Some said one thing, others said another. They didn't know what was to be done. They didn't really know what I had. It was my heart. It would seem like I was getting better and then I would get bad again. It was such a struggle. How I suffered! And I was getting thinner. My mother suffered so much. All my family thought I was going to die. They all suffered.

And so I would go every day to the doctor, and finally the other doctors said, "Well, we just don't know." Later they found a serious infection. Oh, I had terrible pains in my bones. I didn't eat anything. I would eat through injections and I would eat through my nose. Just horrible pains. How I suffered. And so when I saw that I was dying, they brought me the Eucharist.

But obviously God had future plans for you. It's important for the people to know just a bit more about the suffering God gave you as a preparation. Things got even tougher. You had anemia and paralysis. Did they not even tell your mother at one point that you would not make it to the afternoon?

My whole left side was paralyzed—my eye, my leg. I couldn't see out of my [left] eye, only on my right side. And so they told [my mother] to prepare everything. I don't know what happened. I couldn't eat. It was just incredible, the whole situation. I knew that I was dying. I knew that life was leaving me, and I didn't know what to do.

At that moment something happened, which I know for the world is impossible to believe. It's something very strange. I realized that the Lord lives among all of us, that He depends on each of our gestures, each of our actions—each one of us. He depends on our health and our lives, on our hopes, our dreams. He depends on our sickness, and He waits for us to look at Him. His eyes—

how they penetrate! It's like radar [the way] He penetrates you with His eyes.

I felt such a heat entering me. I felt a vapor, or something like that. Very, very incredible. All of a sudden I sat up. I just felt the strength. And all of a sudden everything moved and the clock fell to the floor. My mother said, "Earthquake! Earthquake!" She came running. They thought I was dying, and the whole building was reverberating, and everything was just making noise, and then in that moment I just sat up with such strength and I said, "Please bring me a light and put it on, and paper and pen for I need to write."

It sounds like the Lord was showing His presence. It sounds like you were seeing Him.

I was like dying, but I don't know how I did this. I wrote something down, and the message said, *"Maria Esperanza, My mother and I will heal you. Do not become desperate. You will have peace and relief from your sickness. My Father has heard you and He will lift you up."*

It was incredible. It was incredible.

You still had health struggles after that. They still thought you might die, but obviously you made it.

I don't know what happened, but I just couldn't hold the food down. They sent me away from my house, and I went to the home of a lady I loved very much, Donna Carmen. . .very beloved of my family. . .very beautiful, too, with her children, her daughters and sons.

She brought you to see a special priest, and he, too, had a prophecy, did he not?

He said, "Maria Esperanza, you are going to get better. Your life will be a miracle. Your life will be a constant miracle." And so he gave me his blessing, and he told me to start over, start again, a new life. "Now you'll begin to be a woman. Now your eyes will open to life. And the Lord will follow you day and night with His mother, carrying you and guiding you with His hand. Listen to them. Listen to the inspirations which you will receive. Obey them and be faithful to what they tell you." He blessed me and left.

I prayed and prayed. My love was Mary, and I loved her most because I felt her pain. I would tell her, "Mother, I want to turn my life over, to become a religious. I don't know how to do that. If I am to live, if I am to become a mother, I want to offer my life in the arms of your Son."

Well, my Mother, I touched her that day, and she told me, *"My daughter, when you begin your pilgrimage you will have many sufferings. They are the pain of this Mother. Help me. Help me to save this lost world, to save Venezuela, my daughter. To Venezuela will come many days of shadow and darkness, days of need."*

So you were sick a while longer but began to improve, and you continued to have communications from Heaven?

Something happened to me that I can't tell. But, anyway, something beautiful happened. I received a beautiful message which I have in my mind, but I cannot say it here. It was a very beautiful message about Venezuela and about our world here, a very, very beautiful message about humanity and about the future.

We'll get back to that and other messages pertaining to the future in a while. You have much you can say about the world. But to finish our introduction here, you recovered?

They made me eat a whole lot of grapes. I don't know why, [the doctor] told me that grapes are great for people who are fragile. When I was there one day he said to me, "Maria Esperanza, you are not sick. No, you are a doctor of souls. You have come to fulfill a mission."

It was around this time that your charisms became known?

People began to come to me, and I actually began to see their souls. I don't know why. When they came to me, I could see their souls. I just don't know how it happened, but it was beautiful, something wonderful which happened in my life.

Maria, in a moment we'll move on to the other phenomena, especially the messages and what happened at Betania. But first, a few more details on your incredible upbringing. Many times we don't appreciate the benefits of suffering.

It was a preparation, truly a preparation. Many souls began to look for me, to come to my house. And actually they were generous, the graces. My sensitivity as a person, or my psychological state as a person, it wouldn't be good for me to tell the world the intimate details of my life. My Lord Jesus never told anything about Himself. He let others speak of Him. My mission is to spread His Word to the souls, to people, to nations—a word of spiritual comfort, of help, of hope.

We know you don't like to dwell on your own phenomena, but we appreciate as much detail as possible. Let's go to 1954, around the time you entered a convent, wanting to be a religious, a sister. If you could tell us about the occurrence during which you were pinched in the hand.

One day when we were there in prayer, On October 3, 1954, I saw from the altar—when Mass ended, there was something incredible that I felt. I saw Saint Thérèse of the Child Jesus. She threw a rose to me, and this rose, I tried to catch it, just as I had done when I was five years old. But it was a fresh rose. It happened that it pinched me right in my hand, and I saw blood start to come out of my hand.

I got very scared, and I felt at that moment that He told me I should not be here anymore, that I should go to Rome to see the Holy Father, because the Lord wants me in the world. *"You will be a mother."* And they sent me to Rome. I didn't know what to tell the sisters. It made me ashamed. I felt very bad. I cried a lot. It was very difficult, but I had to go.

You were still being prepared by Heaven for your mission. What happened immediately after?

The following day when I arrived in Caracas, it was another feast day. I went to Holy Mass for three days and went to Communion. I had to prepare for three days, they told me, until October 7, which is Our Lady of the Rosary. So I went to Communion for those three days of Mass and prayed, because Our Lady wanted to possess my heart, which of course was something very strong and very emotional for me. It was very, very difficult. They left a test for me. I lost all my faculties, and for several days I felt like I was very ill and dying. Afterward I went to Rome. I stayed there until December. And afterward I returned, and the following year they sent me there again.

Years before, as we recall, a confessor told you that something would happen, and the same was told you during apparitions of saints such as John Bosco, correct?

John Bosco announced to me that on November 1, 1955, I would meet the desire of my heart—my husband. He announced to me that I was going to meet him this day, and I thought it was a joke, because I said, "No, I don't want to get married."

It was a battle. And so they sent me. And I left again. The first day there, they recommended to me a monsignor before I had left, and he recommended me to another monsignor who worked at the Vatican secretariat. I told him that I was going to try to stay there in Rome and look for a place in a convent.

But God had other plans for you and persisted in them. On November 1, 1955, you met Geo, your hus-

band. Obviously we can't go through every detail of your unusual life. But before we get to the apparitions and messages, a few more personal details. You met Geo and were married in the very chapel dedicated by the Pope to the dogma of the Immaculate Conception. How did that come about?

On the 13th of October, the Blessed Mother told me that I had to be married on December 8. And it was wonderful. There were some guards at the Vatican and my husband was working in Catholic Action and also worked there, and so we had access there, and so they gave us permission. Afterward we came back to Venezuela.

You traveled extensively through Europe and learned to respect other faiths.

I don't deny anyone his own faith. I respect the faith of all people because you just follow what your parents teach you. I think we all go to the same source, but through different fountains. And so, why do we all fight against each other?

While in Italy you also had conversations with Padre Pio. Did you not also experience a transfiguration into Padre Pio when he died?

That's very important. I was here in Venezuela. There was a chapel in this house and it was around 7:30, during Mass, in the evening, and I saw him. He said, "Esperanza, I have come to say good-bye. My time has come. Now it is your turn." The priest and my husband saw the stigmata in my hands. I cried the whole evening, and the next day I saw in the news that Padre Pio had died.

Yes, on September 23, 1968, a day we should honor. When he was alive, how many times had you met with him?

So many times. At first when I was in Italy, monthly. Then he told me every two months and every three months to visit him. He told me, "My daughter, look for a spiritual director in Rome so that he follows your steps.

So I am going to recommend to you Father Felice Capello of the Society of Jesus." And really Father Capello for me was like my own father. In the most difficult moments when I had to make decisions, he was like a moral support to me, spiritual support. He taught me to know souls better. He taught me to understand others and to feel in my heart the fire—the flame—of Jesus.

Little by little things began happening...

CHAPTER 3

The Middle Years: Mary on a Hillside

Obviously the following years were filled with the chores of any wife and mother. You have six daughters and a son. As everyone who meets them knows, they are themselves beacons of light, radiant in spirit. We'll be hearing from them later. What we'd like to know now concerns the apparitions in Venezuela. Throughout your life you had private visions, locutions, and apparitions, since you were a child. They were very private, but that changed in 1976, didn't it?

On the 25th of March, 1976, was the first apparition [at Betania]. For me it was something very beautiful, and it has really left in my heart the flavor and the grace of the heavens.

There were various apparitions which took place. First, March 25, 1976, afterward 1977. There were two apparitions in 1976—on March 25 and then August 22 of that same year. Afterward, in 1977, when the Blessed Mother appeared in the grotto, she asked of me and called to me. The day was incredible because we saw a great light from the doorway at the farm that went up to the sky. A great light—it was incredibly bright that day, with the presence of my Mother in the grotto. Afterward, some time passed, and she reappeared and continued to appear. It was very beautiful, everything, because there in Betania, with the presence of my Mother—with her call, with her grace, with her splendor, with her gentleness, with her tenderness, with her sweetness, she called us so that we would come there every Saturday and Sunday if it was possible. And we fulfilled this request of hers exactly. And there were abundant fruits through the conversion of hearts.

The four sacraments took place. There was baptism, then there were many people who were confirmed, many people who received First Communion, and many marriages. It was a very difficult job for all of us because we had to look for all the people who were poor in order to prepare them and to help them for this event so that this event would be something which would remain in the hearts of everyone who heard of it and experienced it.

There were about nine apparitions in this period, from 1976 to 1984. The majority of the apparitions that I have of the Blessed Mother, I didn't put them down on paper because I think it's something for me privately. I don't put everything down.

The Virgin had told you many years before what the land would look like, before you secured it?

Our Lady told me it would have an old sugar cane mill, a fountain or a rock where water flowed, a grotto, and there she would have her apparitions. And just as she said, that's what happened. When we bought the land, at first I looked at the river, the house, and the sugar mill and I said that it looked like the Jordan. People would be baptized in the river. And we bought it and then I went to Rome and we spent two years there. It was when the Virgin told me to come back to Venezuela, then she was going to come here on the 25th of March, and I came here and then, just as she had said, so it happened.

How many were with you?

We were about 80.

You were in Rome a lot in between?

This was 1974, and that same year I went to Rome because it was a holy year. We spent 1975 and 1976 there and then 1976 we came back for the apparitions and then I went back to Rome in July and August for vacation. And then the 28th of August she appeared again in Betania.

It is intriguing that "Betania" means "Bethany." What else about the first apparition in 1976?

That was 8:30 in the morning. I had been preparing for this and the messages she gave, they said the waters would be like the waters of Lourdes and heal the sick and that the sick would be alleviated of their pain so that people could live a life more peaceful and serene. This was the holy fountain of Betania. I was in front of the grotto [once] when all of a sudden, I was staring there, looking at the grotto, and I saw like a white cloud, enormous, beautiful. Then a friend said, "Maria Esperanza, the farm is on fire, the farm is burning, like a candle," and I said, "Yes, I see the fire," but it was from there that the Virgin and the cloud came.

And when she revealed herself, she went up to the top of the tree, and I saw her beautiful, with her brown hair, clear brown hair, dark brown, her eyes that were light brown and she had very fine, very pretty eyebrows, tiny mouth, a nose very straight, and her complexion was so beautiful, it was skin that seemed like silk. It was bronzed. It was beautiful. Very young. Her hair was down to here, to her shoulders.

And the hair, she had a veil that flew in the wind and among the trees. Her mantle flowed in the wind. Everything was full of light and her hands were outstretched and from her hands came light. Everything lit up. The people said they saw the light. I couldn't see it.

That's when she gave me the message of her reality. Her coming was a reality for everyone to see and feel—so that she could really carry her message to the world, and so that mankind would become conscious and would really be able to live life honestly and as Christians, in a dignified way.

We hear many reports of the Virgin appearing elsewhere. Are some of these visionaries false?

(Maria smiles slightly and knowingly but says nothing, giving a nearly imperceptible nod and showing a twinkle in her deep brown eyes.)

There are reports of her in Medjugorje, Yugoslavia. Did she ever say anything to you about Medjugorje, about whether it was true she was appearing there?

(Maria nods.) She said, *"Yes, but my little ones will suffer."* She said it would be *"a test of love."* The war will not go on forever but will require outside intervention before tensions wind down.

Back to where we were: the Virgin began appearing at Betania in 1976 and 1977, which was about five years before Medjugorje. Why do you think she is appearing at Betania?

These apparitions are a call from our Mother to mankind so that we will really become conscious of our actions and responsibilities, so we will become sensitized, more sensitive. In these times we really need a change. We need changes in the way we live and behave, and especially that all of humanity meets one another and becomes unified. Brothers must meet brothers in a dialogue in which they can understand each other mutually and they can arrive at an arrangement of peace and love among all men of good will. This, I think, is why the Blessed Mother is appearing.

She is calling us and imploring us. She is the Mother of God who comes to evangelize, and this evangelization brings the reconciliation of men and of nations, because already it is time! It's time that mankind realizes why he is living. This living nowadays has become an anguish, a continual worry, because we are on the brink of war, and we have to avoid this at all cost.

Maria, we'll get into more details about the possible future war you perceive. What generally is the warning?

She is coming to look for us amid the brouhaha of an

atomic awakening that is about to explode.

You see important times?

Our Lady says it is *"the hour of decision for mankind."* Her call is not only to Betania. Her call is heard in all parts of the world. She's appearing in all parts of the world so that in this way, all together, all of us united, will form within our hearts the flame, the light, the fire of love of her divine Son, Jesus. She appears in many nations so that these nations hold hands with each other.

Jesus is knocking on the doors of our hearts through the request of His mother—so that, in this way, really, we can unite with one another and reconcile with one another and live the Gospel.

Tell us more about how the Virgin appears, what she looks like.

The first time the Blessed Mother appeared to me on March 25, 1976, was for me something so tremendous it is difficult for me to explain. Nevertheless, it seems to me that living that moment is something that will remain recorded in my heart forever. I saw her in the grotto, in the forest, dressed completely in white—a young figure of about 14, 15, or 16 years old.

She was beautiful, lit up. She looked very gracious. Her eyes were, well, we could say cloudy—they weren't exactly completely black, they were brownish. She had brown hair which flowed at her shoulders. She had a little veil which covered her, and this veil went through the branches of the trees because she began to go up to a very large tree that was there in Betania.

She had a tiny mouth, a smile—how delicate and gentle!—and a very perfect, fine nose. Her face: a little elongated with her cheeks which could be seen naturally colored and rosy. She was beautiful!

And you felt—

At this moment, I felt as if she was saying to me, *"My little daughter, tell my children of all races, of all nations, of all religions, that I love all of them. It doesn't matter—for me, all of my children are the same. There do not exist rich ones or poor ones, ugly ones or beautiful ones, black or white. I come to gather all of them to help them to go up the high mountain of Mount Zion to my fertile land of Betania in these times so they can be saved.*

"So that they unify, so that they will live as brothers.

"I love all of them—the youth, the innocent children, the beloved baby just born. To this youth I am directing myself so that they will really serve me and make me happy, so that they go to the foot of the Cross and continue going through all the world to save the world.

"And that in all of their hearts, hope of the new world continues to grow where everyone can live together, brother and sister, through the love of Jesus, my beloved Son, in the Eternal Father.

"I love all of you so much, oh, so much do I love you, my little ones, that I desire for all men who hear me at this time to receive the grace of the Holy Spirit and make each other happy so that in this way the face of the earth is renewed.

"And with love that Jesus gives to you, you can reaffirm that His words will never pass away, because I leave you a commandment: to love one another.

"Here I am. Here I am. Keep this in your hearts."

And this is the synthesis, the summary, of all of the messages.

That also summarizes much of what she has said at other places. She mentioned particular nations to you, didn't she?

To the United States in the north, that with its strength, with its will, with its courage, with its energy and its desire to be superior, that the United States manage to save Latin America from the greatest pain a mother can have, which is socialism. Socialism destroys the Christian family. *"Help me to carry this cross, my children. I am a mother who wants and asks for justice, who asks for strength of will in the hearts of my children. I love all of these children, even though they forget me.*

"And all of my religious children, all the priests, please love each other and support each other, and take care of the poorest ones and the most needy, the innocent children, and the mothers who are alone and do not have moral support—who don't have a hand extended to them when they are in difficulty.

"And now, all of you who are feeling me in your hearts—come here, my children, to my motherly lap, take refuge in my heart. My heart I gave to you, my heart I give to you, and my heart I will always give to you because I am your mother. I am the Mother of Reconciliation. I am the Reconciler of Nations. I desire for you to become apostles of this motherly heart and to live the flame through the fire of love which Jesus has given to you."

In the instant I received this message—oh, how beautiful, how precious!

CHAPTER 4

More Messages: Door of the Holy Mount

Maria, you often lapse into what's nearly an alternate state of consciousness. You did so just a few moments ago. You lapse into the voice of Mary or Jesus from time to time. Mary seems to speak through you spontaneously. People feel her. At other times you're in semi-ecstasy. Many would find this peculiar.

I don't even know how I start speaking. People tell me that when they see me in Betania—that they don't know it's the Blessed Virgin, but that it's like I am the one who is speaking, but speaking very strongly. I feel like she takes me over. It's a surprise. People say that my face changes, that my wrinkles go away, that I look younger, that I move around like a child, that I sing with a voice that I know is not my voice.

In the U.S., questionable people do this, and it is more like mediumship or channeling. But with you, it is somehow different. There is one account of a woman in a hospital who swore she saw you transfigure into the Virgin. But back to a little history, Maria, you have correctly prophesied certain political events here in Venezuela. You've also forecast events in Rome.

When the Holy Father was going to die, Pius XII, and also John and Pope Paul. When [Pope John Paul II] was wounded, the day before, I thought, "Oh my God, the Pope!" I spent the whole night praying. I was desperate,

I was so desperate, and I was saying, "Lord, how can this be? How can there be an attempt made against his life, Lord?" And I'm thinking, "Lord, who's going to tell him? How can we avoid this?"

And it actually happened, and I spent three horrible months suffering—my stomach, my womb.

It was three months that I spent so sick, and I didn't get better. And I thought that with my prayer, with my sacrifice, with my pain, I was helping the Pope.

From what your friends say, you met with Pope Pius XII, and there was a prophecy handed from pope to pope of a woman who would one day come, and who fit your description. Maria, tell us a little more about your time in Rome and about Padre Pio. Some people even compare you with him.

Well, Padre Pio, for me, was a saint. He was a saint on earth and he continues to be a saint in Heaven. I cannot compare myself with him. He was great. And I hope he becomes canonized, because I knew him, I met him, and I know how he was. The night he died he appeared to me in the chapel here.

And indeed there are similarities between the two of you.

There are graces, yes, special graces that for me, it is difficult, painful to show in front of people because I would like to hide myself rather than be in front of people. I would like to hide myself because for a mother who has a family, for a woman who is older—it is difficult to be before the eyes of the world.

There are many phenomena associated with you, the rose which grows out of your chest, the light which sometimes seems to shine around you.

Yes, yes. I cannot hide them. At the beginning, I tried to hide them, and I tried not to show them to anyone at the beginning. I was ashamed. It makes me ashamed, but lately I have felt that the Lord is telling me, *"All right, now, it's time, go ahead, go before the people."* We are all instruments in the hands of Mary, because she is the Queen of Heaven.

Maria, you have almost surely been given a glimpse of the afterlife. Where do most people go?

We all pass through Purgatory. In order not to pass through, it is necessary to live a very saintly life. Husbands must love their wives in the right way and take great care and love in forming the children. Our Lord lives among us. Our Lady lives among us. We don't see them, but we feel them in our hearts. Silence brings to our hearts the recollection and peace to interact with the people we love.

To live a saintly life in the secular world is nearly impossible. As a result, certain Christian groups in the United States are forming new communities. I'm not talking about survivalist communities, which can quickly turn into cults, but rather Christian-living communities. Do you feel this is a good trend?

Yes, especially in mutual living together, because I think that in a very little while we're going to be living in social communities, religious communities. This is a very important point that you have to take into consideration because the very economic situation of nations and villages—especially Venezuela, which doesn't have resources right now—dictates that they will have to really try to live together, to cooperate with their ideas and in their feelings and intuition and their love and their Christian charity.

In her messages Our Lady says she established Betania as *"a place of peace and harmony to those who will come to search for this mother, shepherdess of souls. I have also come to ease the burden of my sons, the priests. It is they who in answer to my call will have to make my place chosen for these times of great calamities for humanity—a sacred spot where all my children* *will take refuge, to rebuild the walls of the New Jerusalem Triumphant, and where all will have to be saved by the faith, love, and truth of people who call out for justice...*

"Now," **the Virgin said to you,** *"meditate in silence and surrender to prayer to understand and accept my presence among you, especially the religious, my consecrated priests and missionary sisters, that they may enter fully into prayer and contemplation that are so needed at this hour of decision for humanity."* ***Maria, those are strong words.*** *"The hour of decision."* ***It sounds a bit ominous.***

It is the message of a mother for all of her children on the whole planet earth, of all ideologies, of all races, of all nations, because the moment has arrived for us to wake up.

I feel the United States has to save the world. There is nothing else that can be done. All of America, the whole world, has to unite in a block to join with the United States to save the world, because if we separate from them a little war will come right away. War is waiting. It's waiting already to come upon us, especially in Venezuela. They want Venezuela to be like the hook or the lure for all of this to begin.

Our Lady told you that the apparition site of Betania is a piece of Heaven like Lourdes?

It is a place for everyone, says Our Blessed Mother, not only Catholics, but for all, because there should be no class distinctions in nations and religions. *"I call you to this place for a special reason, so that my union with you will be more intimate and vital by the Holy Spirit, allowing you to live the gospels more profoundly... exhorting you to act with generosity and a correct attitude, that Our Father's intention is to save all His children from the mocking and ridicule of the pharisees of these apocalyptic times."*

It is the *"Bethany of a powerful day."* It is apostolic

preparation, being able little by little to overcome many things. The Hell that has arisen among men must be extinguished.

[The Virgin says], *"My message is faith, love, and hope, and above all, it brings the reconciliation among peoples and nations, because it is the only thing that can save this century of mercilessness, war, and eternal death.*

"Arise! The time has come to rebuild the moral values of the people of God."

If one knocks on the door—pounds, insists—the door of the Holy Mountain will open.

It's such a powerful phrase, "the door of the holy mountain." It reminds us of Jesus praying on the mountain. How about Jesus and the way He appears?

In Betania three months ago He appeared to me and I looked at Him but I couldn't really look at Him. I saw Him there, but I couldn't really stare at Him. He was beautiful, Jesus was beautiful. He had His hair down to His shoulders, and afterward, you could see this thing on His head, like a turban, as in Arabia, something that they used to use in the olden days. And He said to me, *"I am Jesus, the Divine Teacher."* And afterward He had His heart there, with blood coming out of it—which was just beautiful. He had the wound on His side. It was bleeding. He had His hands there—oh, I could have died! It's such an emotional thing. I have also seen Him walking like in Capernaum, walking tired throughout Palestine, as if He was saying to me, *"You see Me, daughter, but now it is your time and in another way. It's your turn. You have to do it."* This is what He said.

What does Jesus want of us?

He tells us to be natural, to be very simple, to do what comes from the heart. That's what He tells me. So often I tell Him, "Lord, I would like to be so cultured, to be prepared and studied." And He tells me, *"No, My daughter, you can't lose time studying. You cannot get off track. I will carry you, My daughter. I'll take care of you."* Oh, how beautiful!

You have said that the messages from Our Blessed Mother are very gentle and that those that come from the Lord are stronger. Can you explain that?

Yes, because He is like, I don't know, He is like the flame of cotton *(she smiles)*. It's like He calls us to consciousness. Our Mother calls in another way. She's more delicate.

You've also had experiences with the Father. It's difficult for people who don't know you, or are inexperienced with this level of mysticism, to believe such things. It is said that you were once sent with 72 people to the mountains and a cloud came over you, like the clouds seen often at Betania.

It enveloped me and my friends saw me go up in the air, and that was when He gave me a message. Oh, I think I could've died that day! It was a year ago *[said in 1989]* and this was so emotional. He said, *"This is when the mission begins."*

What's important is that the world converts, that these messages of Our Blessed Mother touch the hearts of men and that the people of God join together. We have to call for the conversion of the people. We have all the tools and weapons in our hands. Only prayer will extinguish the evil, the evils that are leading to destruction of the young.

If we change our attitudes, if man comes to realization and a mind which is stimulated by the grace of the Holy Spirit and listens to the voice of reason and gives a hand to his brother, all men will enter into co-existence, with one people coming to terms with another, one nation with another. They will be able to establish a relationship which is full of solidarity. War would be avoided and so would misery and hunger. Everyone has a hand to extend.

Maria, many look for your hand, hoping for instant miracles.

It is hard. During these days a friend of a lady friend of mine came to me and said that her husband had died and she has four children and she doesn't know how to survive, and she asked me to help her. But I don't know how to do this with everyone. I don't have enough to help everyone. And there are a thousand cases like this. It's so difficult for me. Sick people, sad people—it's so difficult, so you know, I have to have a very good balance in my life and try to look like I am always smiling. But it's hard.

And harder yet, you've been lead to travel.

I've been making a call to the United States. Five years ago I was told by the Virgin that Massachusetts would be where I would begin a mission to the United States. I was told the second visit would be to Canada, and then that I would be going to a big farm. It gives me chills to think of it, because that is what has happened.

Although the apparitions in Betania began for you in 1976, they changed in 1984. On March 25 of that year, not just you but 108 people witnessed the apparition of Our Lady. Why did Our Lady suddenly decide to become visible to so many people?

There have been many apparitions. You can't count them, really. Many people saw her and many people continue to see her. When she appeared to me personally, I felt somewhat badly, like a lot of people were looking at me and they didn't see anything. They would only see the movement of the sun. Or they would see like a white cloud in the forest. And I asked my Mother, "Well, my Blessed Mother, when are you going to come for the rest of your children?" And so she came to me and said, *"I will come for all of my children. Some will see me.*

Others will feel me—feel my presence. They will feel their lives improving and changing. I will make myself visible to everyone on March 25, 1984." Each person who comes here will be heard and helped.

Why do some people see and other people don't?

I don't know. Many people are very good, very religious, holy—they're priests—and they haven't seen her. And there are other people who have seen her.

The first time she came like Our Lady of the Miraculous Medal, and Our Lady of Lourdes, then the Virgin of Carmen—on her knees. The last time she came she looked like a statue here. It was like a movie, just like an old movie in black and white, but she had green around her.

On February 22, 1991, a similar happening occurred down at Betania, did it not?

It's something so difficult to understand. [Christ] came and filled me. He said, *"Go over there to where there is another fountain of water because I am going to give you other fountains of water."* We went and started to get water and when we got there a friend of mine said, "Maria Esperanza, I don't know what's going on. This water is coming out! We don't know where it's coming from! Come here—what should we do?" And so I went—it's as if something told me to. I went there digging in the mud, right there by the sugar mill, and I'm thinking to myself, "What is this about?"

I stuck my hand in the hole. I was covered with water and mud, and it was incredible. I began to play with the rocks and mud, and I wanted to pull out this thing that felt like a rock but I just couldn't. It was very heavy, and there was all this water there, and then I pulled it out. And the moment I pulled this thing out, something great happened. It's emotional for me to say this. You know, it was like levitation, like I levitated.

You received a message from Our Lord, did you not?

He told me, *"My daughter, on the 25th, Kuwait will be unoccupied. For now, do Me this favor. Leave the mud on Me."*

And then we looked and saw that it was a cross—a crucifix—that I had in my hand! And then He said to me, *"I am staying among you so that you will know. . ."*

But it's just incredible, all of this, I don't know how to explain it all. What is certain is that He arrived, and oh! How beautiful it was for all of us there. We all looked—oh! I feel like I'm going to cry. But He said, *"Leave Me like this. Don't wash Me. On the 25th, I will show Myself."*

Well, truthfully, everyone was looking at it and touching it and He said, *"Let them touch Me, let them have Me."* And so everyone was touching it even though it was all covered with mud, and little by little it became clear of the mud and on the back there is something important. It was very old.

Like an antique crucifix left many decades or even centuries before?

On the 25th, when that happened—everything with Kuwait—we were all at my house together, everyone was at my house, and we washed it, and you know, it was beautiful. It was something so incredible. The whole community was there. And Jesus told me, *"My daughter, I remain among you crucified, but I have the hope that My children are going to convert, and it will be the religion of love. Because it is My Love that I give to you. As Catholics you will save yourselves, but I want everyone else from other religions to save themselves, and they must understand My message."*

The whole day was really something. He left me the image of a little crucifix.

What purpose do all these phenomena serve, Maria?

I don't know why these things happen. God only knows. I have no idea.

You are called to evangelize?

Yes, to evangelize. The apparitions are to convert mankind in this time of history, and avoid war, and to call to man's consciousness his moral values.

There have been healings at Betania. Is the water touched by Our Lady?

There have been many conversions at Betania. Yes, that's miraculous. I do believe it's miraculous. Betania offers the world the light of the new coming of the Second Coming of Jesus. A new era of resurrection and a meeting between God and men, with brothers all united. God is requiring this of man now so that man can come to his fulfillment as a light in the world—as people of light in the world.

What message was most important to you?

It was the first message I received. It was after I was ill. And it really touched my heart. I received it on December 8, 1948. It was beautiful. Oh, incredible. I was such a little girl. At the time it was impossible for me to comprehend. But it was precious. It was something so beautiful, something so spontaneous, where Jesus was saying to me, *"You were born in the world, and in this world you will live, My daughter."* He was saying that the world is profane and it tricks mankind, *"but you will help Me to save many if you continue with your faith and strength."*

It was so incredible. He told me everything that was going to happen in my life. He described everything to me.

Allow us to interject another message. Our Lady has told you that we must "fight with the weapons of love." She told you, "Arise. The time has come to rebuild the moral values of the people of God. . . My children, rise,

all of you, to one ideal. Fight for the poorest and for the helpless. Fight for a new generation that must grow and develop. Learn to value each person in the milieu in which he or she moves and lives. You must help them fight the evil that surrounds them. Bring them forward to live in a healthy environment and in peace of the Spirit." We've summarized them and done a little editing, but that seems to be a key message also. Once again, Maria, how would you summarize the meaning of Betania? Why is it occurring?

Because the moment has arrived in which man must wake up in these times of great calamity for the world. The main message is to extend our hands. It is reconciliation. It is to save us from the war, to promote the Word of God.

Man is now asking himself, "What are we going to do to avoid war? What are we going to do in order to unite ourselves?" We learn these things if we turn ourselves over completely, as the Virgin says, to share with her. The manifestation is so all of her children become aware that she exists, and that she continues to exist, and she will continue to exist throughout all generations. Until eternity, she will always be.

CHAPTER 5

"The Moment Has Arrived"

Maria, you said Our Lady is appearing at Betania to make us conscious that we are on the doorstep of war. What exactly do you mean by that?

Well, because now in these times man is full of passions and desiring everything. He's materialistic and he desires everything. And so she has come among us. The Lord is waiting for all of us there at the temple gates.

When the world believes in God and accepts Jesus, loving Him, and loving those who have denied Him—loving everyone—how beautiful will the world be! It will be a paradise! There will not be persecutions or wars or sicknesses like we are seeing now, for example AIDS and so many other awful illnesses. We will live in peace and nature will flourish. It will be resplendent.

Mary has told you that humanity has "deteriorated by the infiltration of demagoguery, falseness, and social injustice," that Betania is "a piece of Heaven" like Lourdes, to remind us of the Father, and that without fraternity there will be a nuclear event and natural disturbances. Our Lady particularly recommends "purity of intention." We must work for the Lord, not for our own egos. We must live in simplicity and humility or else we will face unpleasant events. Is that not what you're saying?

Eventually something will come up. In 1953 I was told things that will happen. Russia will act before the

United States in a surprise way. In 1972 or 1973 Our Lady appeared to me and said she would try to avoid clashes between the West and East, because it would be something very grave—clashes between people and government in the U.S.S.R. and two personalities would arise and one would have good intentions. It would be a very difficult time and tough to have peace. The Virgin was waiting for the conversion of Russia, which would come after a difficult time among themselves.

You say we're on the doorstep of a war. Is it soon? Is it ten years from now? Is it avoidable?

Really, I cannot say. It could be within two years. It could be five years. Because there are things which must remain in silence, since I hope and trust in miracles, in the miracle of the love of a Mother in order to detain the awful conflagration that threatens us.

What is the terrible thing?

That terrible thing is war of—it's a, I can't say it. I can't. It would be imprudent of me to say it.

But you make clear that we can mitigate it.

With the Rosary we can placate the thirst for revenge in men, who want to destroy their brothers through their desire to have material riches. Our Lady begs us to pray 15 decades a day: the Joyful, the Sorrowful, and the Glorious Mysteries.

The Joyful bring the joy of the birth of her Son to save the world. The Sorrowful bring the message of His Cross, and this is one of the most sublime acts of Jesus, at that moment during His last breath when He left Mary as the mother of all of us, as the mother of all humanity. The Glorious are when He rose from the dead. All of us rise with Him. That's what she wants; that's what she told me. The demon is represented in men who are anxious and full of greed and pride and men who steal or kill for gold.

The Holy Rosary is the way. We have to begin to do this so we can overcome every negative force that comes near us. Now is the time of meditation, reflection, and especially of union—true union with her Divine Son.

And with her motherly heart. In union with others. She said to me, *"My little daughter, can't you see that I am trying so hard for this? I come because I want you to be heard. All my children must save themselves. The bad must be stopped."* The Holy Spirit intervenes so that we—man—receive the Grace of God.

What of possible future illnesses? Some believe we face new viruses, new plagues.

Before AIDS appeared Our Lady told me, pray, pray, pray, because an illness is going to be discovered, and there won't be a cure at the beginning, but after they will find a way so that the virus will be contained, enclosed in a way that won't harm. It will be a terrible sickness, and it will come through sex.

That is because people are abusing passions. They have no control. And now [Mary] told me another sickness will come, that the person will only last for a month. How can you avoid this? Yesterday I met a married couple with AIDS. Already I have seen eight cases, but two people have been healed.

There are rare sicknesses emerging that have not been seen before. Every day there is a new virus. Here in Caracas there is a new virus that causes bronchial pneumonia.

The heavenly hurricane will come to help the weak ones, a battalion led by Saint Michael the Archangel, who will defend you because he will announce the decisive time, and he will be open to listen to the drums, flutes, and bells, able to stand quickly to fight with the prayer of the Magnificat.

Something is coming, the hour of terrible things during which confused humanity will not find refuge in the human earthly heart. The only refuge will be Mary. Misery will ruin the nations, sicknesses will cause problems and pain and crying—will imprison the hearts, hurting them without mercy. What pain! There will not be a ray of light to help them, and that is why I plead to you, all Christian families, to get together in your homes and pray. Pray a lot, asking for infinite mercy.

You seem worried about the Church splitting, a "schism."

Unity is urgent, especially among our priests. We have to be more united than ever. This Church is holy, immaculate, perfect, but the men in it can be imperfect, sinners, with weaknesses. Yet no one can destroy it.

But they're going to *try* to destroy it. They're going to attack the Church, attacking the priests to make them weak. That's why I ask you to pray for the priests. They are sacred. A priest is untouchable. They are the points of light in the world.

What else are we told to do?

Confess. Go to Confession. I felt that Mary said this: "Get prepared." I don't know what this is. What does this mean? The impression that it gives me is that we all have to be like children. She is going to perform miracles for us and help us if we find comfort in her arms, but we have to pray the holy Rosary.

Prayer, meditation, penance. Eucharist. This is what she has always asked. It's like she said to me, *"You thought that today you were going to rest, but you can't rest. You don't have a right to rest. You have a right to do good to your brothers and sisters, to serve others. You can't stop, you can't rest even one day, you can't lose even one day. To lose one day is like losing your whole life. It's the sacrifice of my Son. You have to earn it each day of your life. Save souls for me each day. You must save all of them, give them new life, new blood—all my children."*

(Maria, experiencing the presence of Mary during the interview, and overcome with emotion, walks away to gather herself. The interview was at Betania in October of 1989.)

You are seeing Mary, here at Betania, in the forest. Everyone else sees a shape, but you see the Virgin herself. What are you seeing?

It's a crown on her head. I can see it perfectly, above there, a little higher, where the light is. There's a little round light right by the bridge. She's very thin. You see the eyes and the mouth clearly. She has a crown on top.

(Maria lapses into bilocation, like a semi-trance, and the witnesses hear her speaking to a man who needs healing, an American paraplegic named Mark, telling him to stand up. He is thousands of miles away. Later a call to the man in the United States reveals that at that very time he indeed had an unusual experience.)

What was that about, Maria?

There's an energy. There's a very strong energy here. We are very well-accompanied. There's a strength here, a tremendous strength.

Obviously, in such a state, you are called to aid people with your prayers of healing.

Help is a prayer through the mystical body of Jesus for everyone who suffers, for the sick people, for the sad people, the abandoned, the children, especially for those in prison. Because these are very difficult moments, and I say that often it is not so much because they are at fault, but because they had a bad moment, and there is a saying that says "justice for sinners." Just like a difficult moment or temptation might trap you into something, and then you have to suffer for it.

Instead of improving their lives in prison, they increase in their rebellion, they feel disconnected from society and I think that we have to call them to examine their consciences with respect to the presence of the Lord. They should find themselves and look for repentance inside, that they do not suffer this total separation from society, that they begin to work. And the big prisons should be open to the world so they don't feel so isolated from the rest of the world, so they can find God and find Christian values, find God their Father, His Love, what their parents taught them—love their brothers and sisters, because everyone deserves this opportunity. They wind up becoming enemies of society, and they leave jails worse than before.

Again, human unity.

We have to get the message of union for all the nations of the world because we're losing time. All of us have to get together. We keep saying, "Unite, unite," but everything stays the same. This is what God wants, that we should achieve this union.

All of us have to unite, and in this way, we can give a hand to one another, brothers and sisters, with a word, with a smile, with a handshake, because all of this good that we have comes from the Lord, and all the bad, the negative, comes from another source.

That other source is Satan. Many visionaries claim they have been physically attacked by demons. This has not happened, to our knowledge, at Medjugorje, but many other alleged mystics claim physical, bodily assault. Have you been physically assaulted?

(Maria does not seem to indicate so and obviously prefers not to dwell on the topic.) The power of God is so great that He has sent His own mother to defy Satan. The Holy Spirit is acting in us and will fill us with spiritual health, so [Satan] will not be able to bother us and will flee and lose this century. This is why Mary comes.

People like yourself—true visionaries—are sent, along with priests and nuns, to enlighten the world. Yet often apparitions meet with rejection.

There was a lack of moral support at Garabandal and other places. Mary was the first apostle of Christ and He has said, *"Mother, you can help conquer the hearts of all my small brothers so that there is solidarity, because*

I am the Christ of all My children. It's a time of reflection and meditation, especially with silent prayer at night. It's then when I make Myself felt. You should make in your room a sanctuary, and in every room should be a place of prayer."

Each person is a being of light. The Lord gives them this light. God is going to make Himself known in homes.

Little by little man will begin to understand the order of the mystical world and in this way, everything will become full of green and hope—with the sweet glance of Mary working through the Holy Spirit, and with the Father who lives and reigns forever and ever, world without end.

In the following chapters we'll be talking more about possible coming chastisements and momentous events. As you said, the moment has arrived. But before we do, a little more about you and Padre Pio.

I was in Rome with the nuns and met spiritual children of Padre Pio, so they took me there [to San Giovanni Rotundo]. We went every two or three months for Confession there. Padre Pio told them, these same people, that a young woman from Venezuela would come, and they took me to see Padre Pio. "Ah, Esperanza!" Padre Pio said during one visit with Geo. "I have been waiting for you."

Friends in Rome were spiritual sons of Padre Pio. I visited monthly until I got a spiritual director in Rome. On the third visit I told him of the dream of the holy land, that Our Lady was telling me of a holy land where she would come. Padre Pio said there will be a hospital for children and there will be young people from many parts of the world, a holy land. Padre Pio was saying this. Already Mary and Jesus had told me this.

And except that a hospital has not yet been built, Maria, his prophecy has come true, in the way of the sacred land called Betania. Padre Pio was very con-

cerned about the world. He too prophesied a "serious moment." If we don't listen to the call of Our Blessed Mother, what will happen to us?

Well, I am going to tell you something...

CHAPTER 6

Later Years: The Rumblings of Chastisement

It's a crucial time, a decisive time for humanity, beginning now in 1992. It already began in 1991 a little bit, but now the second part starts until 1993, and from there you have to be really conscious so that a war does not explode upon us, because all of us are here to save ourselves.

So God's Justice has already begun and will slowly and gradually accelerate—until it explodes into a chastisement like war, a chastisement of our own making?

People talk of punishments. They talk about the Lord and His mother. They are mercy. They are kindness, love, forgiveness. They will try to allow mankind to regain an orderly way of thinking within himself, in which he will have to suffer little things within his conscience, but afterward he will take consciousness.

At this moment, right now, man is punishing himself through his egoism, through his lack of charity, through his lack of conscientiousness. As a result, we're about to be in a big war, but I have more fears for natural disasters because there are so many injustices in the world and the Lord is making Himself felt by His Justice.

I don't want to alarm anyone. I just want the people to recover so they will have the will and strength to take the Bible and prepare themselves—defend all the rights that Jesus gave us, the right to an honest life. We are people of light. And people of light must be conscious of their duties. We cannot be concerned about money or houses or big cars. No. The moment is arriving when we must leave all those things. This moment is coming.

So in other words, the chastisement has begun and first manifests itself on a personal scale: more illness, more crime and blasphemy, more personal suffering. We think of crime and divorce. God has seen our egoism and is withdrawing a bit of His protection—abandoning us to ourselves. Is that your message?

Man is suffering because he is not conscious of his actions. Our Lord is calling us back to ourselves. Without reconciliation there will be no peace. We've got to know that when the Holy Spirit is there, we cannot fall into sin. We cannot involve ourselves in what is false and lying, nor in conflict with others. We have to be saved. We cannot wait. We have to make friends with everybody. We cannot become critical. We cannot be divided. We must unite and fight against the enemy, and he is very strong.

We already see the satanic war in which ethnic brothers in former Yugoslavia are killing each other, especially in Bosnia-Hercegovina, where the Virgin appears at Medjugorje. How close are we to something even worse?

I'm not going to tell you that we are all going to kill each other, that the world is going to end, that we are going to destroy each other—no, no, no.

They say at the end of this century, everything is going to end. That's impossible. I don't believe it. I believe in the heavens and earth, in the waters, the stars, the moon, the sun—the world!

We are bones, flesh and bones. It's not possible that the world will end. It will continue throughout generations, and this world will continue progressing and becoming conscious and perfecting itself in order to live a life which is really happy, because individuals will have found themselves, because they feel their God and know and learn how to respect Him and to love Him and to love their brothers and sisters.

And so we will arrive at the plentitude, at the fullness of a life which is dignified. We will live a life which is worthy in the eyes of God, a life which is dignified and refined and perfected, with good upbringing, good teaching.

So we are at a crucial juncture of history. Many evils threaten us, and we will face a "serious" moment—a revolution in general—but in the end we will open the door to a better, more God-loving world. That seems to be your message, but many other visionaries are a bit more foreboding.

Perhaps—I don't know—because they say this is going to come, that is going to come. . . I think, yes, well, maybe, yes, some of this will come, but I don't want to think that the Lord is going to abandon us and give the power of the devil to men so that they completely disintegrate. It can't be that way. . .

A very difficult moment will arrive, but there will remain good because the Light and the Grace of the Holy Spirit will always illumine a few people who still desire justice in the world—the truth and the recognition of Jesus with His love throughout all time. This is at least a little bit of hope for people, because people can get panicked.

You have to give to the consciousness of men the message that this world can change, and that everything is going to be in the right way, that it is going to be very well. We cannot go back. We cannot step backward but rather we must take a step forward. We have to go step by step in a balanced way. We must be balanced in all that we do and think. A very great balance. The truly spiritual life requires great balance. The messages are a teaching of wisdom and humility. We must have hope for humankind, for humanity.

But you are not denying a major chastisement?

Our Lady is coming to lighten it. She comes to give us strength, to resist temptations. This is why we have sicknesses in these times: because man has abused the things that God has given us. Man is disobeying.

Here is a message from around March 4, 1989: *"My little children, you see me. Here I am, ready, at the service of all of you who arrive to visit me in search of my fountains of holy water in order to bathe your heads and to purify your hearts, full of hopes, consolations, and spiritual peace.*

"My little children, go forward. The journey is long. It is the pilgrimage of a lifetime, in search of hope, the promised hope of a powerful day.

"My little children, those of you who love my Divine Son are invited to enter fully into our temple of nature, because the principles of love, of human docility, and of Christian fervor will be your guide.

"These are teachings in order that you will understand the essence which is contained in the commandments for new life and founded so that everyone will come to me full of faith and humility, and will come to the heart of this Mother to ask for her maternal protection in order to take refuge there. Mary, Reconciler of Nations, your guide. . .

"And here, that each person who comes near me will be heard and helped, because I am the mother of the hungry, I am the hope of the thirsty and the afflicted who need hope and protection.

"My little children, here you have really come to discern my message and to listen at the same time. In the morning, the song of the birds, being able to see my figure at the foot of the trees by the grotto, the waters flowing over the rocks of the spring, singing to my Lord.

"Oh, my little children, my mystical glance will be

fixed upon every face!

"I can look into the depths of your hearts and see the desire of an interior renewal in order to analyze and contemplate all of the beautiful things which are hidden, which are enclosed in this temple of nature.

"I have chosen all of my children to receive this. My little children, go forward. You will have the ability to understand the heavenly wonders that exist here and with your desire and will, you will be able to take part in the banquet of love that We offer you—my Divine Son and His mother—so that you will live a new life singing to the Lord His songs of love.

"And now, my little children, I recommend to you to pray, saying all the time, 'Blessed are You, Lord. Rest here. Take shelter in my heart.'"

CHAPTER 7

These Times

So, Maria, it's tough right now, the demons are on a rampage, but there's a light at the end of this great dark tunnel?

It's going to improve, the evil in man. People are beginning to meditate and reflect, and new ways will be opened.

Jesus will be present among us. He is making Himself present among us. We will see Him in glory with rays of light. He will brighten us with His rays—the whole world. The last messages are beautiful—the way He will come in glory.

The world will not end but instead, after difficulties, perhaps great difficulties, including possibly a huge war, will purge itself?

This war has a remedy. It can be lessened. We need wisdom and humility.

People say, "Oh, this is someone who studied, someone from high society," and they say, "What do you think, Maria Esperanza, is the century ending? Do we have ten years left to live?"

And I think, gosh, the whole thing is that we have to have our feet here on earth, and to think too much about all these things going on or things that will happen—no, we can't think too much about that. Spiritual things, yes, but the other part, no. We can't spend much time thinking about it.

The thing about Fatima, when they said, yes, there would be a war—this was a reality, and okay, it was over with. But now the Lord is giving us opportunities so that man himself will become strong and will see the light and will see that the world is beautiful. It's precious! Not so that you want to get rid of it—but the opposite.

And yet we are to detest the things of the world, according to Scripture. We know there are trends in world history, good and bad. We know we need purification. Something is in the wind. At Medjugorje the Virgin says these will be her last apparitions on earth, and she has confided secrets, some of which are undoubtedly ominous. To deny them is to negate part of Our Lady's message. She mentions that we are in "special times" and tells us to discern the "signs of the time." Is not Betania a sign of the times?

These are the words of the Lord and His mother: *"You were born in the world, and it is in this world in which you will live, fighting, My little daughter, combating problems in order to win souls to My service.*

"Because the world as it is going cannot continue much longer. Man employs his evil and his astuteness and makes his spirit poorer, and I cannot accept that, since My Heart was given and continues to be given so that everyone will be saved."

This is for the whole world. That's why she's called "Reconciler of Nations." She has to reconcile the world, because without reconciliation, there cannot be peace.

Men must be careful not to test atomic weapons, because there is something in the air and the earth's core is also out of balance.

There will be much upheaval and we will begin to recognize more of it in the middle of 1994. In the midst of problems there will be a large assembly of world leaders.

The Lord told me that [Betania] is the land that was promised for these times of great calamity and spiritual affliction of mankind. He was saying to me, *"The* moment of great difficulty and calamity in the world will arrive." And it is necessary to go about preparing oneself in order to avoid conflict among peoples and nations—guerrillas, soldiers. . .There are pitfalls along the way.

People cannot understand each other, and you *have* to understand each other. We have to help one another to reach a solution in order to avoid a war that would terminate with the deaths of many—millions and millions of people.

The Holy Spirit and the holiness of the Holy Father can open the horizons of a new dawn of Jesus. He's coming. And that's why the Lord wants to get all the minds of men straight, so that they can be saved, so they will trust more in Him than in themselves. There is no perfect person, no living person who is perfect, not while in the flesh.

We're nothing.

Maria, you don't like to dwell on the chastisements, but there is so much talk about it. You recently told pilgrims that you saw a problem with two tall towers, and a month or two later the World Trade Center in New York was bombed. We have all these so-called locutionists claiming there will be the big earthquake in California and such. I realize that no prophet is a hundred percent reliable—only God knows all the details—but what, at this time, do you see for America?

In the next few years the United States will suffer much. There will be problems and certain natural calamities. I see little quakes and certain others. Pray for the leaders of the United States! Pray for the priests in America, especially the seminarians, that they be good and loyal priests. It is important to remain loyal to Rome. People have to pray, to do penance, to meditate very much, and meditate upon the reasons why they have to prepare themselves in order to evangelize. But all of that is accompanied by the Eucharist. *"Because,"* says the Lord, *"only My daily food, if it is possible, will be able to save you from catastrophe."* I have this. All of this is written down.

We paraphrased a few things you've said, not just here but in informal talks to pilgrims. We hope we have it right. What more can we say about the coming justice?

It may come like an earthquake, something like this, very hard things. I see like caves inside the earth. The core of the earth, it is not balanced.

You are aware of the other apparitions around the world?

Yes, yes, in Medjugorje, in Spain—many places, many nations. The Virgin more or less says the same thing. But there are in some of them—it is as if everything ends. And you know, it can't be that way.

All of [the various apparitions] bring about effects. But do you know what is happening here? Here it is not only about what is going to be [as far as world events], but that she asks for seminaries, for help for the old people, houses for children, and for poor people, hospitals—a series of conditions so that people consolidate and unite more. Here, she asks for the people to unite, to work with the truth. This is the basis of what is happening here: for the people to unite and work for the good of the Church.

So like San Giovanni Rotundo, where Padre Pio was, the call for Betania is to develop a center to help people, especially a hospital. Perhaps some of those reading this will donate to such a cause.

This place is a very special place. All of the places where my Mother appears are special because they go to the same source. Since I was young, since I was 12 years old, I began with this. I worked with the poor in Caracas, and afterward, I went to become a nun when I was 24, and after that, when I was 26, I went to Rome. The Virgin told me at that time, in 1954, that this land would be a call to all of her children, a call to reconciliation.

The manifestation is so that all of her children become aware that she exists, and that she continues to exist, and she will continue to exist throughout all generations.

Maria, you have taught people one strong message: that love and humility are what you have called "the crystal bridge to Heaven." From what I understand an angel told you that. Humility, humility, humility. So many believe they are humble and yet exhibit spiritual pride, trying to play one-upmanship. We see this constantly. They become jealous rivals, struggling to see who can get closest to a visionary, or who has the largest prayer group. Or who is the holiest! It becomes like a cult, with everyone judging others by his or her own little standard. And of course pride is rampant throughout the secular society. Is not division a great problem? Have you not encountered such problems? How do you view those who may criticize you or even worry that you are idolized or that you bandy about too many prophecies?

My life is something which I never imagined it would be. People say, "How can this be?" But that's how it is. It's not a lie. My life has been a life in which I have fought with the world, and I've just lived it the way I am—spontaneously and naturally. People who want to pretend like they have humility—it's not sincere. I don't like things that are hidden or false.

There is much love and much forgiveness for those who have doubted me and have hurt me. My human dignity is strong because I think that we are all part of Jesus and His mother. I don't want people to love me but to respect me. Respect. Yes, this is important. I don't ask for anything more than respect. I am just like any other woman. I have attributes and defects like any other human being—naturally. We've all got to improve. We've got to call to ourselves.

You are saying we must put aside all comparisons and differences.

Let us unite together in one heart, in one fidelity in Jesus and in Mary, so that the Holy Spirit will work in such a way that all of us will be converted into fire, into living flame, so that this world grows and hearts continue to be purified and solidarity among men occurs, so that all of us can really live as the Lord asks us.

And this is my message. It is not only for Catholics, and for Christians, but for everyone.

We all have to save ourselves. God wants to save all of His sons.

That was also a key message out of Medjugorje, where the Queen of Peace said we must respect other religions, even if certain religions are more graced than others. We are all children of God. She also sent instructions to the Pope that he was not just the spiritual father of Catholics but of everyone. Do you not agree?

The Holy Father, Pope John Paul II, has touched me so much as Holy Father. He has been so simple, so humble, and he goes in search of everyone so that they convert—those who live in darkness. Just as the Holy Father says, he goes looking for all of his children.

And so I say that when the world and all of us believe in God and accept my Jesus, loving Him, and loving those who have denied Him—how beautiful will the world be!

The environment will be fresh and new, and we will be able to feel happy in our world and in the place where we live, without fights, without this feeling of tension in which all of us live, constantly feeling pressured, living a life that is not tranquil, that is turbulent—a life in which you don't know when you leave your house if you will return.

At least in Venezuela that's what we're living these days in these times.

CHAPTER 8

Dawn of the Son

You are speaking about crime, Maria, societal chaos, and you have also mentioned the possibility of a "revolution in general."

I am seeing that we are like paralyzed. We speak of these incredible things that are going to be happening, and we say, "Where are you, Lord?"

There are many workers in the vineyard of the Lord, but so many more workers are lacking who must carry their weight and carry the Cross of the Lord.

If we carry the Cross with love, we will obtain everything that we want, and war will be ended—countries fighting countries.

I think that my Mother is going to touch their hearts in order to alleviate the pains and burdens of everyone and in order to open their hearts so they fight against this poverty and the difficulties in this world, and the general decomposition of the human being, something which is very terrible in the world.

Yes, we do have to learn, to go to the university, to study, because good studies and background are important, and I believe in all of this. And I believe that when science and spirituality are in agreement, there will not be sickness anymore on the earth. We will all be well.

Our Mother wants us to get our minds straight in the noble and generous ways of life, in all our consciousness. We must improve. We must let go. We must try to be calm. I try to prepare myself so that the Grace of the Holy Spirit can open the horizon of a new dawn of Jesus.

You have a special prayer for us?

This prayer I say every morning. Our Lord taught me this prayer. I say it in the morning when I first wake up: **"Father, I raise my eyes to Heaven and I do nothing but look at You and feel Your Divine Presence among us. In this new dawn, we consecrate ourselves to Jesus, Mary, and Joseph. Glory to God in Heaven—Father, Son, and Holy Spirit, Amen."**

Thank you, Lord. Blessed will be. And then I recite the 23rd Psalm: "The Lord is my Shepherd. . ."

Let's talk about your phenomena. Science could never accept any of the phenomena that occur with you, the glitter that gathers on your skin, the scent of roses and cinnamon from your breath, the stigmata and visions. It seems impossible.

Oh, my Lord, so many other mystical things, marvelous things which would be difficult to describe to the world because man still denies them.

Really, the phenomena taking place in Betania are so numerous and the multitude of little things which take place—the movement of the sun changing colors, the sun which grows and returns to its normal size with colors and all sorts of hues, lit up brilliantly, which fills us with tremendous emotion. Especially the blue butterfly that since I was a child they told me that the blue butterfly would appear to me when two angels appeared by her statue, and that was how it was. They continue coming, they visit us.

Just as also when we are bathed in this glitter, the beautiful delicate glitter which covers our skin, it is beautiful, especially when the sick are cured. Something else that's important is the rain that falls from the heavens on parts of the farm. It's like last night in front of this tree. It was like rain.

Where did it come from? We receive these rose petals and we look around and think, "Where do they come from?" They come down from the heavens!

The bridge to Heaven is love and humility, but also faith. With faith in the love of God we will defeat Satan. When we have faith in God, who is infinitely more powerful than Satan, what can evil do to us? Yet right now faith is terribly lacking, Maria, and you constantly warn of impending war.

I take a look at the Orient and the West. I hope Israel makes peace with the Muslims, that they make peace between them, because there is a nation within those people that may provoke a war—a very great war. This could be very great. And comes Russia, Germany, and then England, and so many nations to defend themselves, and this is going to be a catastrophe.

You've got to be careful of Cuba, here in the States. You've got to. They say [Castro] is dying and he's old and everything, but no, he's got a lot of people behind him. Those people have missiles, and I have a lot of fear for New York.

I cannot talk on other things, but let's pray for your president, that the Holy Spirit illuminates him and puts him on a straight path. He's not an evil person.

And the Orient?

The yellow races will stand up, and that's very serious and I'm very afraid, because they would like to rise. We are living difficult times right now, and I expect an earthquake in Venezuela. We're living them now. A very difficult and serious time will come. There will be a revolution in general that will make people rise up against injustice. The Justice is coming. A very hard moment will come soon, but it will make us better people.

Besides Asia, you worry about Russia, don't you?

Be careful, especially when all seems to be peaceful and calm. Russia may act in a surprise way, when you least expect it.

I feel a great responsibility right now, because something great is coming. Something worldwide. It's a very great responsibility and you have to pray a lot. I'm not interested in you speaking about Maria Esperanza. It's not being humble. There are small things you can tell, little things, but I don't think the right moment has come yet, the right moment to spread something that doesn't belong to me but is from God.

What can we say?

Pretty soon Our Lord is going to give us a test, but it's a good test. It's not a bad test and most of us are going to see Him, to see this event, and it's beautiful. I have all the descriptions of this event! And we're going to know it. It's not going to be the end, and it's going to happen pretty soon. It's going to renew us completely. It's going to be a renewal in which we can really place ourselves, and we can really know what we have to do.

Whether or not we're speaking of the formal "Second Coming," you make clear that Christ will one day soon manifest Himself in a very noticeable way.

There are things that only the Church should touch, and I respect the Church so much. But I am going to tell you something: He is coming—not the end of the world, but the end of this century's agony. This century is purifying, and after will come peace and love. That's why our mother has come to reconcile us. With reconciliation will come peace.

We have to be more united than ever, because Jesus is coming. His coming is near. Perhaps I will not live to see this, but the Lord is coming. Little time will pass. You may ask, "How do you know this?" And I'm going to tell you: Times have changed. Most of the people—not all, but many—are losing their faith. We think we know everything but we know nothing. We need to re-establish this faith as soon as possible.

During one of the interviews you lapsed into a vision concerning this same theme. Mary spoke on the same theme, did she not?

She was wearing a crown, and she said, *"My little children, My heart I gave to you. My heart I give to you. My heart I will always give to you. Little children, here I am, here I am . . .with my little ones who have waited for me anxiously. The children, the innocent children, those who are fed by the Body of my Lord Jesus, my Beloved, and I'm going to tell you what the Holy Mother Church, my beloved son, John Paul II, is giving—the holy touch to his children where he has gone to visit so that conversion will take place . . . so that peace will come about and unity among all those who want to enter the Church. It is waiting for all its children of all races, of all villages and nations, and especially those who search for the light.*

"As I already told you earlier, the new dawn of my Divine Son Jesus."

And how do we prepare?

We have to be very pure and very honest in everything we do, and trust the right souls, the right persons. We must rise to defend the Church through prayer and penance. We have to respect the Church. We have to follow the rules. The world is waiting for a guide, for orientation. The Virgin says to us, you have a mission, and the mission is going to be fulfilled with the demonstration of humility. It will be completed with obedience, with fraternity, and especially with gentleness and kindness, candor and hope in this mother who comes to gather you in.

All of you have to save yourselves. All of you. There is no doubt about this, that you will save yourselves, because Jesus will be felt very clearly in our hearts and you will see Him just as on that great day of His Resurrection and Ascension into Heaven.

The world will stretch out before His majesty and will say, how can this be, this great event, that God came to us?

It will be in a way never before imagined by man, because the Light of His New Rising will be evident to everyone. And of course, man is still not ready for this, to accept these profound things, which actually are so simple and so clear, just as the water which comes down from the spring.

Mary says, *"But at the same time, many, yes, will accept the message and will reflect upon the important parts of this my message that I am giving to you so that in this way, all of you will prepare yourselves—preparation—spiritual preparation for the apostles of my heart.*

"Jesus gave Himself and took from each one of us the most basic men, from fishermen in the village. Some of them were working in the factories of Nazareth, other ones were just farmers, and everyone shared together. Everyone arrived at where they had to arrive so that Jesus could complete His mission as the Son of God who had been awaited by all nations, the One announced by the prophets of the Old Testament.

"And now, my little children, what happens now? Our Heavenly Father, with my Divine Son, they say to me, working through the power and the grace of the Holy Spirit, 'Humble woman of Calvary, the time has arrived in which you are going to gather all the little souls into your heart so that they can become apostles, so that faith is rejuvenated within and they

grow, these innocent ones, these young ones, these youth, full of fidelity to their Church.'"

The Lord came here to Betania—this was on January 22, 1991, in the morning—and there were about twenty of us here, and we were all praying, and there, up there, Jesus came. It was He who walked. He was walking like up above the trees, and He was walking and He called the sheep, and He said, *"I am coming to pasture My sheep."*

It was beautiful. I don't know how to explain it. I felt crazy, but it was a beautiful thing, and in that incredible moment which happened to us (it was two in the morning) I saw Him and everyone saw Him as Christ the King. He had the world in His hands. It was beautiful. It was like He was calling everyone who didn't recognize Him yet.

When we were watching Him I felt Him internally and I said, "Let's go to the chapel," and I felt Him say, *"My little daughter, will these, My children, be ready to receive Me?"*

And so I felt a fear within me, and I didn't know if there would be a scandal or what, and so I went to the chapel, and everyone probably thought, "Why is Maria Esperanza going there alone?"

But He was walking up above the trees, it was just beautiful, and so I said, "We have to go," because I felt His voice within me, and so we all went to the chapel, and this was at two in the morning, and we were there until 2:30 or 3:00. We were there for more than an hour.

And we were praying there in the chapel, and they said, "Oh, the Lord isn't going to be here anymore." And I said, "Don't worry, the Lord knows what He's doing!"

And then in the morning we went back and looked into the leaves and He was there again. And it was an incredible experience. And He said to me, *"Daughter of Mine, when I come, it will not be just for you. All peoples will see Me."*

It was so. . .It's difficult to explain, and even more difficult to believe. He has told me, *"I will come among you and few will recognize Me. I will come among you in a resplendent sun. My rays will reach all nations to illuminate you, to enlighten you, that you may rise and grow as plants grow, with fruits. You all have the right to receive the grace of God the Father."*

Our Lady Reconciler of People and Nations.

Like the healing water of Lourdes, France, miraculous cures are attributed to the cascade that flows at the grotto of Betania.

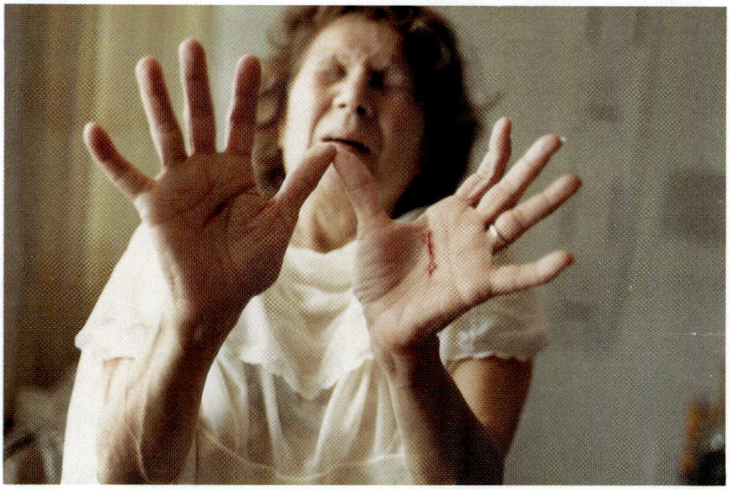

Good Friday—visionary Maria Esperanza suffers the painful wounds of Christ.

Pilgrims often come to kneel before the grotto at Betania to seek Our Lady's intercession.

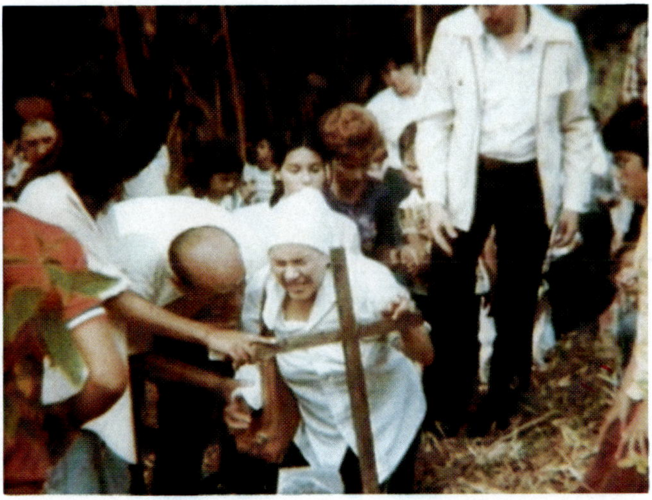

Maria suffers during the Stations of the Cross as seen here in the early days of Betania.

On December 8, 1991 the true presence of Christ is witnessed in the bleeding Host.

Thousands make their way across the bridge that leads to this small piece of Heaven.

Like Zietun, Egypt and Ukraine, reports of visions abound among those who visit Betania.

Many compare the gifts of Italian stigmatist and mystic Padre Pio to those of his spiritual daughter Maria Esperanza.

Bishop Pio Bello Ricardo addresses the faithful as he continues to monitor the events in Betania.

The fruits of Maria reflected in the love of her family.

Throughout Maria's youth she was gifted with visions and many spiritual blessings.

Married on December 8th 1954 in the Chapel of the Immaculate Conception, Esperanza is seen here on her wedding day.

Esperanza and husband Geo seen here with their seven children all of whom today are married.

PART II

The Nature of the Phenomena

CHAPTER 9

A Word from the Bishop

Although at first skeptical, Bishop Pio Bello Ricardo has become a staunch supporter of Esperanza and the Betania apparitions. Here, he explains what happened and why he approved them. He has been bishop of Los Teques since 1977, and was trained as a psychologist. Unlike many bishops, who form a commission to study such events, or who simply ignore them, Bishop Pio took the unusual step of investigating Betania personally. Parts of his pastoral letter approving Betania are reprinted in the Appendix at the end of this book.

It is interesting to me that, as an intellectual, Bishop Pio was initially an adamant skeptic of Betania, virtually antagonistic until he saw the fruits with his own eyes.

Bishop Pio is a thin, older man with a calm and circumspect demeanor. He is more accessible than most bishops, welcoming visitors to his office at Los Teques and allowing those who come to freely record and photograph him. He is a very cerebral man who ponders the more arcane aspects of Betania as he puffs a cigarette. He speaks very adequate though slightly broken English. I have touched up a little of the syntax. His words are a useful glimpse at how the Church evaluates apparitions, before we get to more of the astonishing phenomena.

Bishop Pio Bello, the apparition site of Betania is in your diocese of Los Teques. Can you explain what happened there?

Events began in 1976, one year before I came to the diocese as a bishop. In that year Señora Maria Esperanza Bianchini saw for the first time the apparition of the Blessed Virgin at the farm. She was the only visionary at the time. There were other people with her who witnessed supernatural phenomena—luminous phenomena on the little mountain where the apparitions took place. Afterward she returned to see the same apparitions several times.

[Maria] had private apparitions until [1984]. In 1984 this changed. The apparitions became very public and many other people began to see apparitions. The specific important date in which we can say the Blessed Virgin changed her way of communicating with the privileged was on the 25th of March, 1984.

That day Señora Maria Esperanza had invited a group, a very large group of friends, for a family celebration and Mass at the apparition site in order to recall the day of the first apparitions.

It was the eighth anniversary, was it not?

They were sharing a little lunch after Mass and all of a sudden the apparitions began in the place where the small waterfall is. The first who saw were some children who were playing. They advised the adults, who were sharing their lunch, and everyone ran toward the site. And there were seven apparitions that afternoon. They were short apparitions, from five to seven minutes, except for the last one which took place for about half an hour. During these apparitions the Blessed Virgin said nothing. She didn't say a word.

So all these people were seeing a manifestation—108 people—but no specific message?

She only manifested herself through gestures. She

blessed many people, and she disappeared, and she would appear again. After that day many other apparitions took place and altogether you can say about 1,000 or 2,000 people have seen the Blessed Mother.

That's incredible. It's like Zeitun, Egypt, or Hrushiv, Ukraine, where many saw manifestations. From what we understand, in the first phase there were 381 written declarations signed by 490 witnesses. Is that about right?

We can't say with exactness how many there were because many have seen this apparition but haven't given their testimony. I would calculate, though, about 1,000 or 2,000.

From what we understand, Esperanza's experiences had been conveyed to Rome in 1978. The Vatican was alerted, but there was no formal investigation until after the events of 1984.

Immediately after March 25, I began the investigation of the Church. Until that day there had not been any investigation. I demanded a written testimony from all the people who saw the apparition. In some cases the people gave their testimony on tape and then I asked them to write it. I have about 550 testimonies that are very good proof. Some are collective declarations given by three or four or five people together. And so the number of people who have written their own testimonies is about 1,000. Many others have seen the apparition but haven't submitted any written testimony.

What parameters did you use to evaluate the witnesses?

The same psychology which can take place in a court for a witness before a judge. I study if the person is a valid witness. I see if it is a normal or abnormal person. Second I check to see if their testimony is valid. A normal person can give a testimony that is not valid.

The people who I have investigated—many of them by their own characteristics deserve credibility. For example, a general in the army is a person who has had official jobs and he deserves credibility. A lawyer, a doctor, a psychologist: they deserve credibility because of the professions they have.

There are normal people who may be a bit too credulous, however. Is that not true?

From the testimonies I can detect some that do not seem credible. Some of them are of a mind that is too emotional.

You were especially impressed because some of the witnesses were not believers, correct?

For example, there was an atheist who went to the farm in Betania, and as an atheist he believed this event was just going to be a weekend picnic. He didn't know about apparitions and had no idea there were apparitions there.

And he went to the place, and he was drinking water from the waterfall, and all of a sudden he saw the apparition without any [preconception]. He was not religious. He wasn't psychologically prepared. He had no expectations psychologically. So it was very important, this moment. I have many testimonies of this type. The testimonies are numerous, and it really gives me the certainty that the apparitions are authentic.

When did you begin to believe in Betania?

In 1984 I already felt certain that the apparitions were authentic, but I avoided giving my opinion and my authentic approval of these apparitions [until 1987].

You're a psychologist, right?

I have a degree in philosophy; a doctorate in philosophy, but I've studied psychology very much and the theme of my studies for my doctoral thesis was experimental psychology. My degree was in philosophy but my properly defined degree was in psychology. And when I was working on this I was a psychologist, not necessarily a believer.

Did you ever have doubts about Betania?

At the beginning I certainly had certain doubts about the apparitions. In the Church false apparitions are now abundant. The apparitions of Bayside in the United States, they are absolutely false, absolutely and totally false. Likewise, there are many false apparitions in the world.

One has to be so careful. In the United States the false apparitions are very refined and clever—diabolically clever. What convinced you of Betania?

The first person who started to convince me was the general in the army. This certainly was a serious witness. He is not just like anybody who is absurd or unbalanced. Since the beginning I believed and saw that it was worthy of belief. I didn't doubt the authenticity of them. And a few months afterward, I really felt sure of the authenticity.

What other criteria did you use, besides credibility of witnesses?

The second criteria is the effect which is produced inside of the person—if they have interior peace and virtue within them; deepening of the faith, a deepening of their Christian lives.

The person should be submissive. The person should be humble and God produces this humility in the person. The apparitions have to produce good effects in the visionaries.

In the United States and some other places, there are visionaries who betray an arrogance—humble on the surface but not beneath. That would put you off, wouldn't it?

As Jesus said, *"A good tree is known by its fruits. A bad tree produces bad fruits."* Very important in apparitions is to watch if the visionaries take advantage of the apparitions for their own financial advantage. This is very important.

In these cases, the responsibility is the local bishop's. You went ahead, and without a commission.

I didn't name any commission. I prefer to study this matter personally and not with experts, because experience has taught me that a commission is the best way to postpone a study—if you want something delayed.

Many bishops, especially those of a modernistic bent, seem to have a distaste for mysticism, perhaps because mystical theology is no longer studied in seminaries—replaced by psychology. Before we get into more of the meat of Betania, just make sure we understand the process of Church approval. How does it work?

The Holy See [Vatican] respects the opinion of the local bishop. Usually the Holy See doesn't interfere in these sorts of cases. If the matter is of great international importance, and it has some implications which are especially complicated, it could be that the Holy See conducts its own investigation—for example, the investigations in Yugoslavia.

In my case the Holy See has been informed about the apparitions since 1984 but they never tried to do an investigation. Instead they depended on me according to the information. The only thing they asked me to do was to investigate this with seriousness.

And they insinuated to me, they implied to me, that I should not take any firm position or make any firm approval until I finished my investigation, because there is a danger that a bishop would give just his own opinion.

So after I finished my investigation I sent to Rome my report on the apparitions, and I also sent some photocopies of all the testimonies which I had received up until 1987. I had sent Rome all of these testimonies, and they haven't said anything about my decision. Obviously, they have approved. They have respected my competency and my investigation.

When I arrived at the end of the investigation I waited about three years, approximately three years before officially publishing my judgment. And when I published it I immediately remitted it to the Holy See.

The bishop is really the one competent or responsible for this, and the episcopal bishops can do something if they decide to, and after that the Holy See. But the Holy See has not intervened in any active way in the study of this case. They have just trusted my study.

You traveled to Rome in order to discuss Betania, did you not?

I spoke to Cardinal Ratzinger twice about this. He had no intention of interfering. It was mainly about Betania. I also spoke to the Pope about it. It was a general observation about procedure.

The Pope said it seemed like a sign of the times, the many apparitions around the world. He recommended a book about Medjugorje by [Father Rene] Laurentin. He seemed to me to believe but he was very prudent. My personal impression is that the Pope believed the apparition of Medjugorje was authentic. I explained the apparition [at Betania] and the main message of reconciliation. He said we must be prudent, but that this seems to be a sign of terrible times. The Pope said the Spirit is using Our Lady as an instrument in evangelizing the world.

Many people downplay the seriousness of our times and denounce warnings as "doom and gloom"—an expression that has grown a bit hackneyed. They treat apparitions as an eccentricity or illusion. Obviously the Pope feels quite differently. Yet there is need for great caution; a very legitimate concern that the devil may be playing games. Satan tends to show up where the Virgin comes, to interfere, or perhaps because he is behind certain of them. Has the devil shown himself at Betania?

A few times to a very few persons—terrible figures, but very few times, like a beast, like a terrible beast, like a serpent.

Many apparitionists and locutionists see images of terrible, apocalyptical events, things that in certain cases seem a bit implausible. They see just about every

disaster imaginable, from earthquakes and darkness to comets or the earth moving off its axis. What do you make of such images?

Some visions can be symbolic. A terrible earthquake can be a real message but a symbolic vision of terrible things in the surrounding world.

In other words, what they see as cataclysms can be a symbol of spiritual turbulence—a spiritual as opposed to a geological quake.

We live in a world which is technical, with no faith. We are not living in the Middle Ages, when people accepted apparitions. Now, even bishops and clerics are against apparitions. But here only two bishops in Venezuela were against Betania, and there are 36 or 37 bishops in Venezuela, counting auxiliaries.

You make a point that your pastoral letter approving Betania was especially strong, that it was not simply a statement saying that the messages were in conformity with Church teachings, but that you took the extra step of declaring them directly authentic.

The last declaration of this kind was in the case of the apparitions [Beauraing, 1932-1933] in Belgium. Generally the bishops don't take responsibility to declare an apparition authentic. They are just reduced to declaring that the content of the apparition is in accordance with the faith and in accordance with the doctrine of the Church. But I have dared to do more. I have dared to declare that these apparitions are authentic, that they are true apparitions.

And that is all it takes, unless the Vatican objects, for a formal Church approval. Will Betania be marked with a shrine or monument?

I want to build a church but not big because I think the people want to see the place of apparitions.

You want to keep it simple. You had no qualms about your approval?

Actually I didn't see any difficulty in declaring

something which seemed to me so very certain. The testimonies gave me such certainty about the authenticity of the apparitions. Other apparitions have been approved in other forms, in their orthodoxy, in their content. But approved in their *authenticity,* this is the only apparation since 1934 (editor's note: the actual approval of Beauraing came in 1949) which has been approved in this form.

Even when an apparition is authentic, as at Lourdes, fake, false, or even diabolical visionaries arise. Dozens of false ones swarmed to the grotto of Lourdes, and now we see a wave of dubious apparitions in the wake of Medjugorje. How about Betania?

I am sure that in Betania, there were some false visionaries. I have been able to detect a few of them. For example, from the beginning I thought some of them were just imagining this, or it was just a fantasy. But this was just a very few people, and certainly there have to be even more people than I have noticed, both having authentic apparitions and imagining them.

The only phenomena which I have witnessed. . . something which happened to Maria Esperanza. I saw the phenomenon of profuse sweating and perfume coming out of her, a perfume like roses. And I perceived it clearly. It was sweat, but it was sweat which had the smell of roses.

I have also been able to see the transfiguration which happens to her when some gold spray seems to cover her hands and face and her body. It is a little thin film of gold spray.

It is very frequently that she will announce things about surprising facts. Also the phenomenon of levitation has been taking place. I have testimony from many people about the transfiguration which takes place in her, the phenomenon of stigmata which takes place on Good Friday. I have also seen that the Host will be floating in the air.

But the strangest phenomenon of all is the phenomenon of the roses. It seems she was chosen in a special way by God to have so much to do with roses. It seems that even petals of roses fall from her body, from the sky around her, from her hands. Petals of roses fall from all over.

And the phenomenon 14 times of a rose arising from her chest. Two physicians sent testimony saying the rose came out of her skin. There was a hole and a bruise and great suffering. The two physicians thought it was a heart attack.

A fresh rose, fresh as the morning with dew on the petals.

You can't even think of an explanation psychologically for why these things happen. I mean, why would a rose begin to grow from someone's chest. What natural explanation could this have?

I frankly can't see any possibility of an explanation for this phenomenon, and other phenomena take place of the same type which definitely have to be supernatural.

Yet your approval of Betania was not a specific approval of Maria Esperanza.

The apparitions at Betania are one area, and the personal phenomena happening to Maria are another area. I have not made a statement on the apparitions and the supernatural phenomena happening to Maria because they seem to me to be two very separate areas. I made my statement on the Betania apparitions only.

Why do you think Maria experiences these other phenomena?

There's no rule to explain why. These phenomena are given freely by God. A person can be very holy and not have any extraordinary phenomena take place. Saint John Berma, a young Jesuit, had not one single extraordinary supernatural event take place in his life. [On the other hand], Saint John Bosco had such a great number of supernatural phenomena happen to him. God can give these extraordinary gifts to people, and it is a charism. It is a gift from God. If a person is not virtuous, it is a sign that these phenomena could be simply psychological, or of an origin that is worthy to be studied in psychiatry. You should always find these extraordinary phenomena with someone who is a holy, holy person. It's more valid.

Once more, we get back to humility, what Maria said she was told is "the bridge to Heaven." When humility is lacking in a visionary, one must cast a wary eye on that particular seer. As for Maria?

It seems to me that Maria is a very, very good person, a very good Christian. She has a prayerful spirit. I would like for my own self the spirit of prayer that she has and the union with God that she has and her constant contact with God. For her there is nothing strange about spending a whole night in prayer, all night long in prayer. She stays awake until two or three in the morning praying, or wakes up at two or three and prays for five hours, until eight in the morning.

She is a great loving spirit, too. She is always willing to help, to collaborate, and to give her helping hand to others. She is a great working spirit also. For me there is something great about her, which to me is like proof of her normalcy—she has such an intense spiritual life, but at the same time she is such a good mother and cares for her house so very well, and her children, and loves her children so very well.

She is a wonderful cook. She is a very good baker. She cooks wonderful pastries. She comes alive in her house and lives her vocation to the fullest.

The impression I have about these phenomena is that they are indeed supernatural. I have no reason to believe that they are caused by some psychological abnormality in her.

The Church doesn't really rule on specific visionaries but rather on apparition settings and stays away from

totally endorsing any particular mystic. Does the Vatican know much about Maria?

I have advised them about her personal phenomena. Last time I was in Rome, I informed them about this personally.

Some might be troubled by the glitter that falls, or the way Maria communicates messages from the Virgin, which often resembles what they call mediumship or channeling.

It is very curious. It is kind of similar to spiritists. It is like she is possessed by a peculiar force, and she speaks or writes the message. But I am sure it is good, not evil. She feels it is not her that speaks, and that is why it seems a little bit like the phenomena of a medium, but it is not exactly the same. She is not physically constrained or anything, but just internally compelled to transmit the phenomena.

As far as I can see, all the results from Betania are positive. The people have received a great impulse to their faith and have been converted. People without faith feel faith begin to grow within their hearts. People who are in danger of losing their lives and their souls find themselves again in Betania.

The Virgin of Betania does not leave as many messages as at some places. Is that an accurate statement?

Here, the center of the visit of the Blessed Virgin is not the message. Here, it is just her presence itself, her visit itself. Very few people have had oral communication with the Blessed Virgin, perhaps five percent. Say about twenty people from about 1,000 or 2,000, in total, have had some verbal communication. Some people have received messages which they said were secret and they didn't want to reveal them.

What has happened is a strengthening of faith here, conversion, growth of Christian life, frequency of receiving the sacraments, prayer, especially Mass and the holy Rosary. The messages don't have anything very distinct or very peculiar or very different from what the Blessed Mother's teachings have been in other apparitions.

On December 8, 1991, an incredible event took place at Betania, the Eucharistic miracle. Blood came from the Host! What is the significance?

One must say that a miracle is above all a sign. It is a signal in which God makes visible something which is [normally] invisible. He makes present something which is absent. He makes touchable something that cannot be touched or seen with our eyes.

The Eucharistic miracle makes visible to us something which for us is mysterious—to know the real presence of Jesus Christ in the consecrated Host.

There are few miracles of this type in the world, and we have had the fortune of God deciding to give us one of these miracles here in Betania.

There is no possibility the miracle could have been faked?

It is possible that false representation of the facts can take place or that someone can confuse a miracle with a chance happening, but in this case it is not so. It was not a coincidence because a Host cannot drip blood. This is physically impossible.

I had a scientific investigation take place, and this investigation was done by a laboratory that is totally trustworthy. This laboratory is the central laboratory, the most important one for the judicial police of Venezuela, and it was the Department of Legal Medicine in this police station where the investigation was done. They did it to see what the substance was that leaked from the Host and they proved definitively that the substance that leaked from the Host was human blood.

Finally, what meaning do you draw out of the entire Betania experience?

That God would like to use the Blessed Virgin again as an instrument of regeneration in a world which has lost its contact with supernatural values.

The shepherds found Jesus Christ in Bethlehem with the Blessed Virgin, and the wise men found Jesus Christ in the arms of the Blessed Virgin. This takes place here in Betania. Many people once again find Jesus Christ through the Blessed Virgin.

This is what is most important, to conceive the Blessed Mother as a pathway and not as an ultimate goal. She is the road which leads us to Jesus Christ. She is an intercessor, an intermediary who brings us closer to God.

The apparitions are a call to reconciliation. It's very good for people to come from all over the country, from all over the world, to reconcile themselves at this place with God and among themselves—under the protection and loving glance of Our Blessed Mother Mary.

For my part I invite everyone to visit this place and receive the grace of God our Lord.

CHAPTER 10

Sign of the Divine

We move now to Geo Bianchini Gianni, Maria's ebullient husband, owner of an oil maintenance firm in Caracas, hardly ever without radiance and a smile. He is a lanky man with a strong chin and patrician countenance. Geo, did you know of Maria Esperanza's spiritual gifts before you married her?

No. I had only one opportunity. There was one time in which she read some sentence to me from a paper that she had, and in those words I felt that she had something, that there was something interesting in her besides the human part. And that was a point that gave me much trust in the moment that I decided to marry her.

How was it when you realized what her mission was?

This happened about twenty days after we were married. I had the opportunity to see something in her that I had never seen but which I believed immediately. I didn't have any doubt. And since that moment something has opened up for me. It was a new horizon.

Geo, you were very spiritual even before meeting Maria. You worked for the Church. Have you always been dedicated to Mary?

Yes, yes, since I was young. It's certain. I was born on her day, December 8, which the Church has proclaimed as the feast of the Immaculate Conception.

Maria seems to have everything in fairly good perspective.

She is a woman of marvelous balance. It's something absolutely incredible.

Yet it also has to have its difficulties.

It has not been easy. Unfortunately, in the face of these supernatural phenomena, there are many people who do not have that balance and they become fanatical. They want to possess whomever they come in contact with.

We have seen the same with the visionaries from Medjugorje. Many have tried to possess them or idolize them, which is extremely harmful to the entire cause. They should not be put on a pedestal, nor bothered too much. In a way, you're a seer. You've seen Our Lady, true?

Yes, on March 25, 1984, in Betania. I gave my testimony about it to Bishop Pio Bello of the diocese. It lasted three and a quarter hours, during which the Virgin appeared seven times, ten minutes to half an hour each time she appeared, and when she left you could see her go away. Three times I saw her disappear. Her image just vanished. It gave you the impression that there was this strength that sucked her out of there.

I saw her three times. Other times I couldn't see her perfectly because I was distracted. But it was something beautiful, beautiful. I felt well. I didn't go crazy about it. I just felt happy. I saw her from about 100 to 200 meters away.

There were other people who were just ecstatic, and everyone was happy that they were there.

What did she remind you of, Geo?

I saw her as the Virgin of Lourdes, Our Lady of Lourdes, with her blue belt. Everything was white. I didn't see her mouth or her eyes or anything. I saw her image at a distance. I could see a little head near one of her shoulders which I thought was the baby Jesus. I felt a great inner peace, a great excitement.

Why do you think she is manifesting herself?

I have concluded this: that the Virgin has come . . . to

unite a small group of souls called for a great future mission, which is already beginning. That is the evangelization of the world over again. To evangelize will mean to make new examples, the renovation with a heart of flesh, not stone.

We need many Saint Francises—many of them: saints on the inside, and on the outside, natural, simple humans, full of love for their brothers and sisters who are suffering.

This in general is the reason the Virgin has appeared in Betania. She wants us to change our lives and respond to her call. We put ourselves fully at her disposition and at her service. God is gathering His children in the whole world.

Geo, you're a normal, successful man, a businessman here in Caracas, what they would call an aristocrat, not the type given to supernatural escapism. You are sure you have seen things with your wife?

After the apparitions other phenomena have taken place of which people have benefitted. They're very interesting, especially things that come from within her.

After I began to read the messages of Maria Esperanza I found a great divine sign in her and around her. She was a woman who had come and had been prepared for something great, which we couldn't even measure the limits of—of what God put in her. And so, since the first message, God—or rather Jesus—the Virgin—told her that a prepared land would arrive to her at the opportune time, because Jesus the Lord gives everything with perfect punctuality when it's ready and when it's time. The things of God are accompanied by the appropriate conditions.

Tell us a little more about finding Finca Betania.

We decided to buy the land because we just fell in love with it and the environment. Everything was beautiful.

We did not realize—we had no idea—if it was the land we were looking for or not. We didn't think about that. Afterward the farmer, he brought 150 cattle to this land and he thought that we were going to have milk production here.

So that you see, how things of God come about. They arrive when we aren't thinking about them. And unexpectedly, like this. Everything was fulfilled, all the conditions, the appropriate time, and that's when she came to earth.

And on that day in 1976 the Virgin made Maria Esperanza understand that this was the promised land—"promised" in the sense that it was promised to Maria Esperanza.

It is a bit like God calling forth His people from the oppression of the Egyptians. He's calling us to spiritual refuge. There has even been a pillar of fire seen at Betania, and other phenomena.

I don't think I'm a fanatic, but I believe much in divine manifestations. I don't have any doubt. I have come to believe very much in these divine manifestations.

The important thing is to come to understand this and to arrive at Betania with your souls ready to understand the vibrations of Heaven.

We must be so careful not to idolize or improperly showcase a visionary. We can admire the great mystics, but such admiration must never turn into adoration, which is idolatry. But let's talk a little more about your wife's gifts.

Well, the talents that Maria Esperanza has, I can give you a real testimony for her gifts because I live with her daily. I tell you that there are phenomena, marvelous phenomena, but these phenomena are to be used to help many human beings who need comfort, who need consolation and help, so that something awakens within them. And so that the force of evil in their lives is destroyed. Maria Esperanza has been called to renew and to wake up hearts that are sleeping so that they learn that God is the only reality of our existence, the only reason for our existence.

You have heard of the apparitions in Akita, Japan; Kibeho, Africa; and Medjugorje, Yugoslavia?

Yes, yes. I am very conscious of them, and I believe in all those apparitions. I really believe that at this time in the history of man and earth, the Blessed Mother is presenting herself in all the countries of the world. She presents her call so that we reflect before it's too late. Which means there is something that is too late. So that means that there will come a time when it will be too late.

And what must we do before it's "too late"?

Love each other. Think about how you behave with other people. Think about it and change.

And really it means that there will come a moment when there will not be any more time left.

With Betania there is a future mission for the whole world which is associated with it.

I'll repeat what I said before. It will be a new renovation in human beings, so that they can transmit to others what they have inside of their hearts. Words are not sufficient. The example is what is important. I have to be an exemplary being in all ways.

Undoubtedly, at the moment of Judgment, when the worldwide judgment will come, everyone will answer for his own life. But no one will be able to say that they didn't know anything about the new evangelization, because this has to arrive everywhere in the form and in the way that the Holy Spirit inspires it to happen in that moment in every person.

We must prepare ourselves and learn to wait. The biggest task which I have come to understand is to convert within, to transform yourself. I am ready to lose everything in order to gain everything.

A personal question before we conclude. You have seven children?

We had seven children in eight years—six daughters and a son.

Your marriage in the Immaculate Conception chapel at the Vatican was very unusual.

I was very surprised. I didn't think it was possible. I knew Rome and the Vatican very well. And I knew it would be impossible. But for Maria Esperanza it was so easy. Of course, having the Blessed Mother at her side, there would not be any door that could stay closed in front of her.

What would you like to convey to the world in closing?

Like I was saying before, you have a great responsibility. The people, the world, must know that God is close. This has manifested itself through the Blessed Virgin in Betania.

We have had experiences of her. We have her and continue to have her. We don't want to seem like special people. We're the same as everybody else—exactly the same, with our defects, with our errors, with our failures, with everything. But we are people who desire a change, a real change in man's existence on earth.

God will feed us. He will give us the strength to keep living our lives. How beautiful it is around us. The life of God, how beautiful it is!

CHAPTER 11

Other Voices: The Daughters

Your name?

My name is Maria Auxiliadora Bianchini de Leon. I am a professional singer and a daughter of maria Esperanza.

Tell us what you saw on March 25, 1984, during the great apparition.

When I looked at the grotto I suddenly saw a brilliant white figure and her dress was moving and so at that moment I felt a chill through my whole body and like my legs were shaking.

And at that time when I was standing there like that, the Blessed Mother, the Virgin, disappeared.

Then everybody went up to the grotto and we began to pray the Rosary and then suddenly the same Virgin began to appear to us, always above the grotto, and when I saw her I fell to my knees, crying. It produced great emotion in me. It was like a fear of what was unknown but at the same time a great and sincere happiness. And that day she appeared seven times, from 3 p.m. to about 6:30 in the evening.

Some of the apparitions were longer than others?

The last time she appeared was about half an hour. We saw her very firmly there. She was right there, and each time she became clearer and more detailed.

And that night I just couldn't sleep, because I felt like she was going to appear next to my bed. I felt very full of emotion and really very happy that all the things the

Virgin had given to my mother, these prophecies had taken place.

I felt a change, a very big change in my spiritual life, a confirmed faith, a more alive faith, a bigger promise.

I would like people to change themselves and convert their lives, as my life has greatly changed.

Yet being a daughter of Maria Esperanza's, such phenomena were not totally unfamiliar to you.

In my house I have seen many phenomena, but they have been in my mother. All of the manifestations and the graces that God has given to her, like stigmata, the rose, the scent of roses—many things and miracles, things that people think could never happen and then with a word from her it happens.

How would you interpret the message coming out of Betania?

I think that the main message of Betania is hope and love. A great change of life is what the Virgin is asking of us—an interior reflection about our lives. Much meditation and above all, much love.

She asks for reconciliation. It's always worth a fight for the positive things in life. Well, what does it mean? It means that you have to really enter into the spiritual life—not only going to Mass, or obeying the Commandments, but you have to really feel this flame, this love, this love to serve God. You have to feel this burning within you.

Now we go to another daughter, with the name of her mother, Maria Esperanza. Maria, what did you realize during the apparitions?

I realized how many people fight for the Church, like my mother, Mother Teresa, and the Pope.

It's an important message, because many people do things that are more for their own ego or superficial holiness—for their spiritual pride—than a suffering

work for the Lord. The apparitions brought this home to you, didn't they?

I realized that in that moment that there has to be something more, and it was like eternity. I felt eternity within me. All of us were hugging each other and kissing each other. It was like discovering eternity.

At the beginning it was like she changed from one style of the Virgin to another. In her right hand she had like a torch, in her right hand, and afterwards I saw her as Mary the Helper with the Baby Jesus.

And then I saw her as Mary seated on the throne with her Baby in her lap.

And then I saw her as Mary, Reconciler of All People and Nations.

Then I saw her as Mary, the Virgin of Lourdes, and when I saw her as the Virgin of Lourdes, I went closer to this area and I realized she was just a huge figure.

And when I went close, it was just enormous. I couldn't even see the top of her, and I had a chill through my whole body, and I saw that her mantle was flowing in the wind, and my hair blew in the wind at the same time.

It was just overwhelming and I had to just go back because I couldn't handle the emotion.

And so?

I went backwards. I went back to my spot. And I saw how she was big. It was something that gave me peace. It was just incredible. It was wonderful.

Let's have a word on the idea of reconciliation. What do we mean by this message?

If you're not getting along with someone, you might think there's no solution. But if you deeply realize what your faith is about, if you look for the positive things, you realize that things make more sense, that the problems will make more sense, and you'll be able to find solutions.

We have to be natural in all of our manifestations of life. We have to be full of hope and happy. We have to hope for a better world, and to make this better world come about, we have to give of ourselves, to give to others, to feel what others feel within our own selves.

We go to yet another daughter named Maria Coromoto. You, too, saw the Virgin on March 25, 1984. It reminds us of some alleged apparitions in Ireland—the grotto, the veil blowing in the wind. What else did you see, Maria Coromoto?

Her mantle was flowing in the wind, going forward and backward, and I didn't see her face perfectly because it was so brilliant. Her outfit was so white that her face seemed sort of dark, hard to see. Maybe it was sort of light brown.

But she was very beautiful. You just felt like you had all your hair standing on end, all of your skin.

And I smelled such a beautiful scent of roses.

Have you seen solar miracles?

I've seen phenomena of the sun, spinning, as if it was going to fall on us—very, very brilliant and spinning. And it turns blue. Then I have seen colors in the sky—pink, yellow, and purple. All of a sudden I would see a person all lit with purple.

You could hear voices coming from the rocks.

The message of Betania is that God is present, God is alive. God is in each one of us.

And now for Maria Gracia. You also saw a manifestation at Betania during one of your mother's visions, including I believe in 1977.

There were about 15 of us together and the Virgin appeared to my mother. This was above the grotto. And one of the persons screamed, "Maria, Maria! The farm is burning!"

And when we looked up, the cloud opened up, and a light came out.

Well, it just blinded me. And I went to my knees and I felt this force push me, and I tried to look, but I couldn't.

And then I saw my mother. I saw that my mother was looking up so peacefully, and she looked so beautiful, and tears were coming down her cheeks. And in that moment she had the phenomenon of levitation. It was just beautiful!

Do you have any doubt whatsoever that you really have experienced the supernatural?

There is no possible way to doubt this anymore. There is no possible doubt about this. And it's a great responsibility. It is not the time to keep quiet, to be afraid, to think that people say you're a fanatic or crazy. No, it's time to say truly, the Virgin has come to us. Everything that the Bible says, everything that the priests told us in their sermons, everything that the sermons tell us—it's true. And it tells us why we're here in this world.

When you come to this place, when you step on our ground, the land here, your life, even though you do not feel this, changes.

And now we hear from you, the last daughter we will hear from, Maria Inmaculada, of whom we spoke in the introduction, as Maria's first born. What was it like to you?

I don't know how to describe it. But it was so beautiful. I think it's the most important thing that's taken place in my life. Now, it's not just a matter of believing, but it's a certainty that God exists. You can be in a desert and if you have God, you're not alone. You're filled up. You feel protected, loved, cared for. God always loves you.

How is it to be the daughter of Maria Esperanza?

She's super-special. She has many gifts, and as she herself says, she also has defects. But she has so many gifts. I don't know how to express myself. You have to know her. She gives of herself. I tell her, "Mom, people are always bothering you. You can hardly breathe. You don't have time for yourself." And she says, "That's my mission."

There's a love which comes from her, a love which comes from her very self. She doesn't ask anything of anyone. She just gives.

What are some of the more remarkable occurrences?

She has received Communion from Heaven. This I have seen.

What do you think is meant by "reconciliation"?

The greatest desire of a mother is to see her children respect each other, love each other. Even though there are differences in religions, there [must be] comprehension and understanding. There must be tolerance—tolerating others. It's union with the Virgin, union with God.

And that union, through love and humility, is the bridge?

It is the intimate prayer between you and God, between you and eternity.

CHAPTER 12

Friends, Doctors, and an Incredible Cure

One of the most fascinating aspects of Betania is the quality of observation. A number of Betania's greatest adherents are the kind who normally shun the supernatural: men and woman of a scientific or journalistic bent. Take, for example, Dr. Vinicio Arrieta, who was director of the School of Medicine at the University of Zulia (and also educated at Harvard), or Samir Gebran, a cellular biologist with a doctorate in immunology.

Or Dr. Vinicio Paz, or Dr. Alfonso Gutierrez Burgos, or General Jose Luis Tarmerosi, or Father Otty Ossa Aristizabel.

One of Maria's son-in-laws, a well-spoken man named Carlos Marrero, worked for a large multi-national advertising firm and told me he was speaking with Maria Esperanza one day when suddenly she fell to her knees in ecstasy, and in her open mouth, on her tongue, he saw a white spot materialize and grow before his eyes into a Host.

Let's start with a few comments on the extraordinary things seen by Samir Gebran, who after visiting Betania ended up marrying Esperanza's daughter Maria Gracia. Dr. Gebran, why is science so closed-minded about paranormal occurrences such as those seen at Betania?

You are asking me about how I could explain these phenomena, and it's very difficult. Scientifically it is difficult. I think that there is a barrier between this [field] and other [fields,] and we as scientists cannot study this because we don't have the instruments to do it.

In other words, we are in four dimensions, and if there exist others, we don't have the instruments in order to be able to show it. Right now science cannot enter into this realm, and that is why, speaking scientifically, I cannot demonstrate this type of phenomena. I know that they exist because I have seen them and had very many opportunities.

What occurrences are hardest to believe and comprehend? What are some of the more extraordinary phenomena that you yourself, Samir Gebran, a man educated in the hard sciences, have seen?

I have seen how petals of roses appear, how there is a materialization of roses, and one smells the roses in the environment. I have seen how the Eucharist materializes on the lips of Maria Esperanza. I cannot give any explanation, because, in her, many supernatural phenomena take place. The fact of believing in God is an act of faith because we have no way of proving it. This is outside of science. Science studies what is tangible, what is before your eyes, what is before the five senses. But beyond that, it is very difficult.

I am a scientist. I have a Ph.D. in immunology, and I have seen the Blessed Virgin of Betania.

These are vital points, Samir, because although it is very narrow in what it can prove and understand, the field of science and those who work in science have unfortunately boggled us with their technical jargon and arrogated themselves above the supernatural. They don't admit to anything they can't explain, and they denounce the supernatural dimensions that are beyond their electron microscopes. Do you agree?

One of the things which hurts me most is to see my

scientific friends and co-workers [try] to find the answer in science, because through science there are new discoveries—the frontier of discovery opens through science—but it is difficult through science to explain the philosophy of life. One can be very intelligent but not have the wisdom of understanding the philosophy of life.

Samir, what else have you seen in the way of inexplicable phenomena?

On the 14th of December, 1985, I decided to go one day to the farm Betania. I spent the whole day there waiting for Maria Esperanza, and since it was late, I decided to go back. At that moment two or three cars passed, and I felt that Maria Esperanza was in one of those cars. It was like an intuition. So I returned and just saw her and I said, "You are Maria Esperanza?" She said, "Yes, I am."

We began to walk toward the grotto and at that moment she began to see the Virgin, as the Virgin of Guadalupe.

And what I saw was a form of the Virgin. I didn't see her very well. I just saw reflections of light on the foliage. At that moment the others were praying the Rosary. Maria felt that the Virgin was telling her to go to the river and get this rock, and so she went and got this rock. And she turned it over. She pulled it out of the ground and turned it over, and it was the same as the Virgin that was appearing—an image of the Blessed Mother on that rock. It was white and there was such an odor of roses. She still has this rock.

Afterwards she received a message, and after the Rosary she opened her hands. She was close to the altar, and rose petals appeared on her hands.

In other words, this was a very special day, and beginning with that moment, my life changed completely.

Why all the phenomena?

The purpose is a means which God uses, I believe, to hook people, to make them react a little bit, to make them realize that there's something different, something besides the material world.

Above all I have seen the conversion of people who have come to this place, to be able to share with us the presence of the Blessed Virgin of Betania and of Our Lord Jesus Christ.

Moving to another scientist, another medical scientist, Dr. Arrieta. Let's start off right where it counted the most to you. Doctor, you were cured at Betania, miraculously healed, weren't you?

I had cancer of the prostate, which metastasized in the lumbar column, spinal L5. And the PSA, the prostatic specific antigen, was 100. The normal value is 0 to 10. I had 100.

You are certain of the diagnosis?

There is no possibility of a misdiagnosis. I am a doctor. I studied two years at Harvard. I built a hospital, which is the one we have now at Maracaibo. I was the director of a school of medicine. And so you will understand that the diagnosis had to be very certain. I looked for the best specialists in the city for this, and they had given me two years to live.

So what happened to you at Betania?

I had gone through two treatments with chemotherapy. On May 12 I made this vigil of the Virgin of Fatima. I spent all night praying to the Lady. I was sweating a lot and it started to rain very strongly, and I felt bad. So my wife, Judy, and my cousin were trying to protect me. They made me lie down, and I fell completely asleep.

At three in the morning, since it was a vigil [now May 13], a group of youngsters arrived, singing a song which is my spiritual song: "May Christ Jesus the Lord Live!"

During my prayers I continued to sweat and then I went back to sleep.

At four in the morning I woke up again, and again at

five. They woke me up with the same song. I was resting in a sleeping bag and I put my face down against the ground. I began speaking with Jesus. I said, "Lord, here you have me, just as Paul of Tarsus, who was thrown from his horse when he persecuted the Christians. I am throwing off my pride. I am throwing off my pretentiousness in thinking I am better than others. I know that my days, only You know when they will end, but I would like a little more time because I have two children who I don't want to leave. They are younger. They are going to begin at the university."

We got up at six in the morning and we broke our fast at seven, and we sang a little song to the Virgin. At eight in the morning the solar phenomena began. There were about 5,000 people there and the solar phenomena began in which the sun lost its light—it was illuminated but it lost its light. The center part became green.

It began to spin on the inside like there was a circle on the inside and then it began to come nearer to us. For me it was exactly the same as the phenomenon which had occurred at Fatima on October 13, 1917, which proved to the world that the Virgin did appear at Fatima to the little children.

I began to feel an infusion, a heat within my body. I grabbed my wife and I began to scream. I can't say it was anything but a scream because even my companion said that I just began to scream. They thought I went crazy. I began to scream, "I'm being cured! I'm being cured! I'm being cured!"

My wife began to wipe my sweat away and she said that I was very pale and I looked very bad. And I said, "No!" I felt an infusion of healing within me.

I felt that this infusion arrived to my spinal column and to my prostate. I wasn't even looking at the clock but after this the Virgin immediately appeared above the trees and toward the heavens as a real human being. That is to say that she had hair which was moved by the breeze. She had a face, an extremely beautiful face, a beauty that cannot be described!

The only thing that can be said is that it is like the expression of love, of the glory of God.

Her eyes are blue. Her nose is very sculpted. And in her face there was a candor, a love, a kindness.

And in her right arm she had the Child Jesus, as if to hand Him over.

And in the other arm a rosary that hung down to her knees. The rosary was completely illuminated. It wasn't like a pearl, but it was extremely illuminated.

Her glance was lit up and it arrived at my body just as it did to some five hundred other people who were seeing the Virgin at that moment.

I thought that certainly I was cured.

And you were!

Five days after that, the prostatic specific antigen was not detectable.

One of the specialists, Dr. Vinicio Paz, who made the original diagnosis, said there is "no scientific explanation" for what happened to you. They did a biopsy which was also now negative. The cancer simply vanished. Another doctor, Alfonso Gutierrez Burgos, tells us of a little girl who had severe leukemia and didn't have any signs of it after visiting Betania and drinking from the spring.

By 1987 there had been around 500 people who received cures. In his pastoral letter [Bishop Pio Bello] defined them as acceptable from the psychological point of view and also the point of view of credibility. Actually, currently, more than 10,000 Venezuelans and non-Venezuelans have seen the Virgin, and the cures are more than 1,000—more than 1,000 that have been documented.

All at Betania. It reminds us of the feeling at Medjugorje. You can feel the peace at that place, can't you?

When you cross onto this land, everyone perceives spirituality. Betania is Heaven on earth.

It's sure seems like a little piece, at any rate. It certainly seems to have made you happy.

It's the happiness of the children of God.

CHAPTER 13

The Wounds of Our Lord

Besides documenting miraculous cures, doctors and other competent witnesses have played a role in observing the phenomena affecting Maria Esperanza personally, such as stigmata, the odor of sanctity, bilocation, and eruption from her body of the rose.

These phenomena especially defy our logic and imagination, at first serving to cast doubts on everything, for they may seem too bizarre.

Yet there are more than enough capable witnesses, the type not prone to exaggeration, deception, fabrication, or hallucination. Not even collective psychosis could account for the strength of numerous testimonies.

Whether or not any specific phenomenon is true is something that has to be treated on an individual basis, but taken together, give or take a few claims, there is no doubt *something* is happening.

For instance, you, Dr. Alfonso Gutierrez Burgos, are you personally satisfied that Maria suffers the wounds of Christ on Good Friday, or at least did for many years?

When I observed the stigmata, the day I observed the stigmata in Maria Esperanza, the general was there and other people as well, so I am sure that these things are happening to her and are of a supernatural character.

I know it is very difficult for other people to understand and accept this, but those of us who have faith and believe in the deeply profound mysteries of our religion believe that they are supernatural phenomena.

You saw one case in which a person had no way out but a liver transplant and yet was healed at Betania. I believe it was a male patient. Could you tell us about this?

I had the medical history in my hands. There was no remedy but to do a liver transplant. He was in a critical state, with varicose veins in his esophagus, vomiting blood. He never used to pray but the doctors in the hospital told [his mother] to take him to Betania, and when they went to Betania, they talked to Maria Esperanza.

Maria Esperanza was seen attending him. She began to pray very deeply and after that prayer she said, "Don't worry. You are going to go through the operation. You are going to find somebody who will donate a liver but you will not need an organ transplant."

They got the means to do the operation, and after many hours of operation the surgeon came out and the mother went up to him and asked, "What happened to my son during the operation?" And the surgeon said, "Something very good has happened, because the liver that we were going to put in your son's body *wasn't as good as your son's liver* (editor's emphasis)."

I examined the wound of the operation and I checked the post-operation reports and I followed the case step-by-step, and I have the proof that all that has happened is true.

People see things and are cured at Betania whether or not Maria is there. In other words, things happen when Maria isn't around, yet one cannot deny her special role. She has even helped doctors, correct? She helped a psychiatrist who had serious headaches.

Maria looked at him and said, "Please sit down and tell me what happened to you when you were 12 years old. Of course, you have to be truthful."

And the psychiatrist said, "When I was 12 years old I hit my head very badly."

And she said, "Well, that is the cause of your pain. You have to pray with me and from now on you will not have this pain."

Sounds like another unorthodox cure, Dr. Gutierrez, and one more case for the record.

The majority of people who have gotten close to Maria Esperanza have been skeptical, especially those of us who are doctors. But we find in her a series of phenomena that have no explanation—no natural explanation and perhaps not even a scientific explanation.

We have no other option but to declare that it is in effect a quality that unites her with divine nature and which causes these spiritual gifts in her to be obvious.

They cannot be pretending. In her is something so real, so tangible, that we can't explain it.

So we must affirm without a doubt that in her a supernatural phenomenon is occurring.

Yet Maria doesn't advertise many of the mystical happenings?

She is very reserved with things that happen to her. She doesn't like any publicity about her phenomena.

And what of the spectacular stigmata, Dr. Gutierrez?

One of the things that called my attention as a doctor to this situation was that on Good Friday [of 1989] Maria called me in the morning because she wasn't feeling well. She had very, very profound pains and cramping in her hands and on her right side and in her feet.

I told her that I was going to come and see her, and so I came here around three in the afternoon.

I found her quite weak, sweating profusely—covered with some type of brilliant substance on her body.

And it was obvious that she was feeling very sick, and she had her hands closed.

Then she opened her hand and I saw that there were wounds on her hands similar to the ones that we call stigmata.

She had these on her hands and also on her feet.

And I was *very* curious.

As a doctor I examined her hands and I tried to see what kind of a wound it was.

They were very fine wounds in her hands and they were swollen in the middle. They separated her skin and they hurt her very much.

That was accompanied by a loss of blood, a tremendous loss of blood, and she told me that in those places where she had the pain, this is where the wounds appeared. Three or four days later I could see that the place where the wounds had been were completely gone.

I would say that there is no explanation for these wounds.

I know she couldn't have done it to herself.

Finally, a journalist: Carolina Fuenmayor, who works for Venevision, a large television station in the city of Caracas, which is larger than Chicago. Carolina, tell us what you saw.

It was Holy Week. I never thought I was going to see [something like the stigmata]. Maria was going through the Stations of the Cross, and then I saw her hands. I couldn't believe what I was seeing. But it was there and I saw it. She was suffering a lot. She felt pain. And I saw blood in her hands. She had holes in her hands for three or four days.

Which led you to conclude that—

Maria Esperanza is a very, very special person. She's not from this place. She's like in-between.

And?

I began to, you know, investigate this case. I went back to Betania a few times. And then every time I went there, I found something different.

The first time I went to Finca Betania was in 1987. The first day, we saw very special phenomena that I hadn't seen before. The whole place turned to different colors. First everything was yellow, then it turned blue and red.

Tell us about the time you saw a manifestation of Mary at Betania.

The Mass, it was going to begin. We were aware that it was going to begin. Then people started screaming, "The Virgin! The Virgin!" My husband, who doesn't believe in anything, turned around and I did too. And it was so amazing. I started crying and saying, "Thank you. I am seeing you. I am seeing."

Believe me, it was beautiful, and so bright.

What did it feel like?

I can't tell you what I feel. It was the most beautiful, wonderful experience that I have had in my whole life. And since then I feel secure, comfortable, and I think I understand now what I live for. I have something important to live for now.

As a journalist, can you still be objective?

Covering this story, I keep my objective point of view, because I have to do it that way, like the priests that conduct the investigation.

Without a doubt, Carolina, the most difficult thing for us to believe is that a rose has come from Maria. This would imply a level of mysticism that is far beyond that of your average "visionary." It harkens back to the level of mysticism experienced by the likes of Saint Joseph of Cupertino, Saint Francis of Assisi, or Padre Pio. Many will use it to try and mock or discredit Maria. Tell us your experience.

I was with her the whole time because we were taping and I was looking at her. When we were coming down the hill, where the waterfall is, coming down the hill to her house, she felt bad, she was suffering a pain—you know, like her heart. I thought she had a heart attack. There were two doctors. One of them took her pulse and said, "You are very bad."

And then we got to the house and she sat down. She was suffering with those pains, and I stared. She opened her blouse and I saw this little rose coming through her chest, and I saw how this rose came out of her chest. I couldn't believe that. Lots of people had told me about it. This was not the first time. But I couldn't believe such a thing, yet now I saw it.

You have video footage of that?

I have footage, but she told me not to show anyone until she dies. The Church never really makes any statements on people like Padre Pio or Maria Esperanza until after their deaths, so we have to be careful how we approach that subject matter.

What happened when your station aired your story on Betania?

You can't believe what happened with that program. A lot of people called me from Maracaibo, from all the states here in Venezuela. And they said a lot of miracles occurred while the program was on.

How did it affect you personally?

I began to need and to love prayer. I go to Mass every day I can. The Eucharist: the importance of receiving God as often as I can during the week, not only on Sundays. This has been quite a radical change, because before, this wasn't important to me. I never thought I was going to go back to the faith that I lost a long time ago. What had been important to me was that I would be famous and I would have a good career. That's what was important to me. But when I went to Betania, I realized the truth: that I should help my neighbor. And we have to be very humble in life and have respect and love for God.

This message is an urgent message. It is! Because the Virgin knows that awful things are going to happen to the world if we don't change. And she comes here to tell us to change as quickly as we can before we lose everything. We should be apostles.

I realized that the only thing that mattered to me was living in peace. It wasn't anything about TV or anything like that. The only thing was to live in peace with my family, and to love our neighbors. This is the message she is leaving for us. She says that humility is the crystal bridge which leads us to Heaven.

CHAPTER 14

"Look! The Host is bleeding!"

Just as impressive as the stigmata, and for some people more so, was an occurrence on December 8, 1991, when a Communion Host began to bleed real blood during Mass at Betania.

The celebrant during this miracle was Father Otty Ossa Aristizabal.

Father, you're the priest in charge of Mass at the makeshift church near the grotto, while they build a new facility. What kinds of phenomena, before we get to the Eucharistic miracle, have you yourself seen?

There was a man who had three types of cancer, prostate, in his stomach, and in his blood. He was just a disaster medically speaking. And he had a cure. He was cured here.

Every week I get testimonies like this. It's very incredible. Last Saturday a lady came with a young girl who had a brain tumor. She was operated on and the doctor told her there was no guarantee that she would be cured, but she was cured. The operation was a success. And when they took x-rays they looked on the x-ray and an image of the Virgin appeared, surrounded by angels. The Blessed Mother was right where the brain was x-rayed.

At Fatima there were three children; at Lourdes one person; in Mexico, Juan Diego; but here she has not just appeared to Maria Esperanza but she has appeared to many people—young people, little boys, old people,

people who are poor, people who are economically well off, people who can't speak or read, and also people who are lawyers, doctors, psychiatrists, engineers, military people. They also have seen the Virgin. I have seen six people who have come in wheelchairs and have left from Betania walking.

Tell us about the great Eucharistic miracle.

Between the 7th and 8th of December of 1991, about 40,000 to 50,000 pilgrims had come. It was just an incredible number of people. It was very beautiful, and the people demonstrated much faith, above all during the Mass. They were full of attention to the Word of God. There was such a silence during the Holy Mass.

I had the big Host that I consecrated, and at the moment of consecration I broke it in four parts. I put it into the dish and I ate one of the parts. I put the other three parts in here [the dish].

I closed my eyes and when I opened them I saw that one of the pieces of this Host had a drop of blood in it, and I thought at that moment it was because of my fatigue. But then when the nun who was behind me said, "Father, look! The Host is bleeding!" I realized, yes, and I covered it. I didn't say anything.

There were so many people there, I didn't know what would happen. They'd kill each other just to see it. At five in the morning I opened the sanctuary and I looked and I saw the Host. The drop of blood was still fresh. And I told the people what had happened.

It was an incredible moment. Everybody got on their knees. Very emotional. I took the Host in my hand and everybody was taking pictures of it. It was very beautiful. And at two in the afternoon I went to take a rest and to give it to the bishop. He wanted it handed over to a medical expert in the institute of Caracas in order to analyze it, and so the Host stayed there for a month at the medical institute and they examined it very carefully and proved that what was on the Host was human blood, that it had magnesium, iron, that it had red corpuscles and white corpuscles. After, I put the Host in the monstrance so the faithful ones could observe it.

Father Otty, what else occurred on December 8, 1991?

Even the water took on this flavor almost of roses.

And conversions?

Jehovah Witnesses have come and would be on their knees in tears.

Which goes back, does it not, to the main message: reconciliation.

The Virgin calls us to renovation of faith, which is especially urgent in a world that denies the existence of God. She asks us to strengthen our faith through reading the Sacred Scriptures, and meditation. She invites us to speak more of God. She asks us to pray for vocations for priests, for conversion of sinners, for peace in the world—the situations which threaten humanity.

This violence in the world is principally taking place because of pride and greed. There is no humility.

She asks us to return to the Eucharist and to have a spirit of solidarity among ourselves to help one another as brothers and sisters, because it's the time for the Mercy of God to be poured upon mankind. It's like the case of Nineveh. Nineveh was going to be destroyed and Jonah intervened to save the village.

And so the Lord says, do penance and move forward.

And if we don't?

I think that the Virgin tells us that there will be a punishment for those of us who are not faithful, to those who try to judge God, who do not answer His call.

He will send us very difficult tests. He doesn't want to condemn our sins, but He wants us to convert ourselves and to live and accept the message of God—to become evangelizers.

Changing gears: what about the devil?

He does manifest himself here, too. He's present. If everyone believed, there wouldn't be adversity. Here, there is adversity. Even Maria Esperanza, she has been persecuted, gossiped about—and even Bishop Pio Bello. They thought he was crazy, they thought Maria was crazy, and me, too. That's how the devil's involved. That's his presence.

But the Virgin has demonstrated that she will continue to be present here in Betania in spite of the adversary.

For me the most important thing here in Betania are the conversions which have taken place. There are physical miracles, but the most important thing is [the healing of] spiritual illness, because there are atheists who have come here who didn't believe in God but have converted. She invites us to turn away from sin to make an apostolic commitment to rejuvenate the faith.

And?

And this is a message for the world.

CHAPTER 15

Afterword: The Fall of Mystery Babylon

So it is that once again Heaven calls to us, and once again it is up to us to respond. Once again we are given warnings about what *might* happen if there is a lack of response. Once more, above all, we are called to love.

And we are called—urgently—to prayer.

As Our Lady of Medjugorje told one of the seers on August 25, 1993, *"I want to help you and call you to prayer. Only by prayer can you understand and accept my messages and practice them in your life. Read Sacred Scripture, live it, and pray to understand the signs of the time. This is a special time. Therefore I am with you to draw you close to my heart and the Heart of my Son, Jesus. Dear little children, I want you to be children of the light and not of the darkness."*

It was the second time in eight months that Our Lady used the expression *"signs of the time"* and we see these *"signs"* not just in the supernatural occurrences but throughout our darkening society. We see them in the rise in ultra-violent crimes, the ravages of ethnic hatred, the anger and lust—bloodlust—in the eyes of our young.

The rise of homosexuality and radical feminism stands as another sign of an age in which demons seem to be spreading their ugliness across the planet. New Agers using symbols that go back to ancient Egypt and

Babylonia, back to the evils of paganism and witchcraft, have infiltrated everything from the Sunday sermon to pop music and the environmental movement. In Salem, Massachusetts, a practicing witch was recently admitted to a league of local church leaders.

Psychics abound, along with satanic ritual abuse and other abominations. Mainstream magazines now use language once reserved for the locker room, and rock bands belt out songs with titles such as "Rape Me." The infamous singer Madonna openly ridicules what is holy by making videos in front of a burning cross or by picturing herself next to Mary and the Christ Child.

It is not hard to know we are in a special time of spiritual tribulation. We see entertainers and priests alike accused of sodomy with innocent children. We see our society transformed into a culture of death. Worldwide at least 37 million babies are aborted each year, and proponents of abortion are now pushing the pill RU-486, which will make the termination of preborn infants all the more convenient. We see Russia and its satellites turning into hotbeds of crime and turmoil.

With such immorality come disorders of a natural kind. The health of whole nations are threatened by cancer and AIDS. Many diseases are caused by pollution. And there is also the spiritual pollution known as pride. Everywhere, there is too much egoism. Everywhere, there is too much spiritual pride. Within Christianity, division continues to spread like a spiritual virus, threatening us with schism, which is exactly the opposite of the reconciliation and unity the Madonna of Betania so ardently and frequently advocates. In France only a minuscule number of Catholics attend Sunday Mass, and in the United States there is worry that the American bishops—seduced into modernism and secularism—will try to split with Rome once the popular and courageous John Paul II is gone.

Signal events such as the Mideast peace accord, which seem so welcome on the surface, ring of further biblical prophecy. We are in a tumultuous time, a time that offers great dangers and at the same time great opportunities. As elsewhere, Our Lady of Betania comes to clear away the satanic confusion. As Mariologist René Laurentin notes, Mary's message at Betania "is counter to the message of Satan, to the work of Satan, and so prayer, union, and utility—the collecting of everything in symbolic reality—this is all contrary to the symbolic and real division that the devil causes in the world with drugs and all kinds of music—violent music—and quite contrary to the symbols of unity which reconstitute us."

Clearly, the time has come for Christians of all denominations to do two things: regroup and love. The manner in which Christian denominations currently carp at each other—believing they and only they have the real Truth—remains a great scandal of our time. Never before has there been so much jealousy, and when such divisions split apart denominations—and split apart movements *within* those denominations—it is all the more threatening to the army of God. Petty differences magnified into significant division are the hallmark of Satan.

The pride and divisiveness in Christian circles must be stopped or Our Lady's plan of intervention, marshalled at Betania and Medjugorje, will fall short, and mankind will meet the forewarned chastisements.

This is the key message of Betania: reconciliation. We must dispel our pride and reach out to those with whom we have had differences. We must expose evil and fight against the darkness but we must do so with consideration and love. We must concentrate on the *good* in people and straighten out the ways Satan has twisted our better instincts. Let me use as an example the environmental movement. What is really a good cause—protection of God's Creation—has been twisted by certain factions into goddess or earth worship. It has turned New Age. This is another hallmark of the devil, to take something good and give it a little twist in the wrong direction.

We were all created good, because God is good, and we must find common ground because we are all brothers. I noted that in the last interview with Esperanza, she acknowledged the skewed direction of President Clinton, fearing he would involve the U.S. in an unnecessary war, but at the same time Maria pointed out the good in him. We need to do the same. We need to know where evil is, and rebuke it, but more than anything we need to focus upon the bright areas of a person's soul and to pray for an expansion of that light—instead of causing alienation.

Hate the sin but not the sinner. Our job is not to annihilate those who have been deceived but rather to demonstrate a straighter path and a brighter Light.

Yet we must also stand our ground. And we must never panic. We are *not* near the end of the world but rather the end of an *era*. It is the final hour of a satanic period. While reluctant to focus upon chastisements, Esperanza acknowledges that we are in this special time. She said 1992 and 1993 would be the very beginning of God's Justice in the world and that events would pick up pace in subsequent years. What has happened thus far? According to the September 1993 issue of *Life* Magazine, "This is how weird our weather has been: The three most damaging climatic disasters in U.S. history happened in the past 12 months. First, Hurricane Andrew devastated south Florida last September. Then, on March 12, a giant blizzard—which the National Weather Service calls 'the single biggest storm of the century'—swept from Florida to Maine, releasing more snow, hail, rain and sleet than any other storm since 1988. Finally, the relentless rain flooding the Midwest brought on what may be the costliest weather disaster of all."

It is as if God is trying to nudge us into realizing that such disasters may occur on a greater and greater scale. Perhaps the first two chapters of *Isaiah*, along with *Revelation* 14:14 and 19:11, fit most closely with our waning era. It is an era of great evil, and the Virgin comes as the woman clothed with the sun to battle the Red Dragon. There is war between the Archangel Michael and Satan. It is a period during which the beast rises from the sea. We are already in a *spiritual* tribulation. Demons have been loosed everywhere.

This Great Evil may well lead to tribulations like those of the bowl judgments (see *Revelation* 15) but if so will be followed by a glorious era, when Satan is bound for a thousand years.

Whether or not we are in the "end times," and whether or not we are approaching the Second Coming, we are certainly in a special period of testing and the entire world has become Nineveh. Esperanza has hinted that while she may not live to see it—she's 65—many may be witness to a great manifestation of Christ. Her constant theme that the world will be renewed—that all will be made new—reminds us of *Revelation* 21.

Christ will reign after the fall of Mystery Babylon.

And so the final word is "prepare." We prepare for all eventualities, and we do so spiritually, with faith, humility, and love. For with those three important components there is no need for any fear. With humility we find the path to our final reward. With love we shirk the spirit of negativism and criticality, reconciling to each other and our God.

So powerful is that message that I expect great resistance to Betania, just as there was great resistance, initially, to Medjugorje. I'm not saying Betania will reach the height of those apparitions, but it certainly has its place, and I have already seen evidence of what may be satanic attempts to quash the messages. The extraordinary level of claimed phenomena will attract a comparable level of demonic attack. I have seen certain cultural traits and family endearments misrepresented by observers who have not yet been close enough to understand Esperanza. There have also been vicious rumors about the bishop.

Again, it is to be expected. It is the test of fire. It is perhaps the demon's counterattack. What will be the final word on Betania? Will the bishop's unusually forceful endorsement endure? Will Betania become another major destination of pilgrimage? Will Maria's charisms stand the test of time and scrutiny?

I'm inclined to think that they will. I'm inclined to think that she is, as Carolina Fuenmayor said, a uniquely powerful visionary—really, a *mystic*—who fluctuates between various realities.

As such she will be misunderstood and maligned.

But if she is true she will rise beyond that, and it will be interesting to see how the matter develops. I maintain my caution until the end. There is much more to scrutinize. If there is any deception, it should be rooted out such that we are not faced with yet another dubious apparition. We must test the spirits (*1 John* 4:1) as long as we do not do so through pride, competition (some prefer other apparitions), or self-interest.

For now I think the greatest miracle of Esperanza is her incredibly devoted family. The more remarkable events claimed to occur around Maria are not nearly as relevant nor as impressive as the love that exudes from her and her family. I've never seen anything quite like it. While some have snickered at the large number of people who travel with her (at one recent engagement there were 77 family members and friends), this is supposed to be one of the best tests of a visionary: devotion and cohesion in the family life. It's the first "fruit." I am in no position to offer a final assessment of her mysticism, but this I can say: never have I seen a mother more loved by her husband and children than Maria Esperanza is.

It will be interesting to learn more of Maria's prayer life, and to hear more of her valuable advice. However dark the times, she says, the victory is ours. The victory awaits our efforts. Heaven awaits our humility and love. We must re-examine our level of meekness and nurture its seeds. We must *feel* it. We must feel love. We must rise to the love of all God's creatures. We must rise to the love of Mary and the saints. We must rise to the love of angels and Our Lord. We must settle down in prayer every day and practice loving everyone who comes to mind, including those who antagonize us—loving their souls, understanding their trials, and ignoring their shortcomings. We must love them, in short, as we love ourselves, and when we do we will draw closer to God.

APPENDIX

Excerpts From the Approval

The following are excerpts from Bishop Pio Bello Ricardo's November 21, 1987, approval of Betania. They begin with a description of the events on March 25, 1984. But the approval is not limited to the events of that specific day. The entire document is 16 pages. It is interesting to know that, reportedly, Maria Esperanza did not think Bishop Pio would approve the apparitions because of his original disposition against such alleged phenomena. Bear in mind that the number of witnesses has increased since the 1987 letter, thus a discrepancy in certain numerical details. We pick up the excerpts after the initial description of the case.

Ecclesiastical Investigation

That same week which began Sunday, March 25 of 1984, the first witnesses spontaneously came to the Diocesan Curia in order to present to me their written testimonies and an oral account of the events.

I received them and questioned them with kindness and broadmindedness, though I had an interior attitude of doubt and skepticism as it is normal for anyone who has had a theological and psychological formation and knowledge of the history of the Church. Even though, due to the quality of the informants and the information they were presenting, I judged the case had to be seriously investigated. To this end I convoked all the witnesses and protagonists; not an easy task, as many of them lived in different cities and out of the jurisdiction of the Diocese.

Due to the circumstances of number and dispersion of the witnesses and the continuing of the phenomena, I decided to undertake the investigation personally. This made it easier to make appointments with the possible informants, something that would have been very difficult to do if I had given this task to a commission.

This option, obviously, obliged me to dedicate a lot of time to this business, around four hundred to five hundred hours; but I could calmly question approximately two hundred protagonists and collect, study, and file 381 declarations. Some were collective declarations. The total number of people that signed these declarations was 490. . .

During my *ad lumina* visit in September of 1984 [to the Vatican] I was received at the Sacred Congregation for the Doctrine of the Faith. I left there a provisional report of the events and was given a document for my private use which was elaborated upon by the Sacred Congregation in 1978, with rules and procedures I needed to follow in order to judge the supposed apparitions or revelations. . .

In the present case, Our Lady has presented herself in different ways, therefore the descriptions vary but are always related to the different Marian devotions: She is most commonly seen as "Our Lady of Lourdes" (because she is seen with a white dress and a blue waistband, some say that she extends her arms out as welcoming or saluting, and with a veil through which you can see her hair) or as "Our Lady of the Miraculous Medal" (probably for the position of her arms and the rays of light coming out of her hands). . .

I estimate to this moment five hundred to one thousand people have seen the apparitions [1987]. What has been usual in the apparitions of Our Blessed Virgin is that those privileged with the apparition besides being very few were poor, not educated and generally children or very young people. In this case there are of course poor; poor, uneducated, but there are also many middle-class professional people such as: doctors, psychiatrists, psychologists, engineers, and lawyers. There are also numerous college students from different universities in Caracas. . .

Declaration and Judgment

Since the beginning of my investigation I realized this was not another case of craftiness, collective suggestion, or a promotion on the interests of a person or of a group of people, but that I was dealing with something serious that had to be investigated carefully.

Relatively soon in the course of my investigation I acquired the certainty that the character of the phenomena was supernatural. Still, I decided to delay any explicit declaration, following the prudent praxis of the Church in these matters. . .

I judge the time has come to make my judgment on the events publicly.

IN CONSEQUENCE, AFTER STUDYING WITH DETERMINATION THE APPARITIONS OF OUR BLESSED VIRGIN MARY IN FINCA BETANIA AND AFTER ASSIDUOUSLY ASKING OUR LORD FOR SPIRITUAL DISCERNMENT: I DECLARE THAT TO MY JUDGMENT THESE APPARITIONS ARE AUTHENTIC AND OF A SUPERNATURAL CHARACTER.

Therefore, I approve officially that the place where the apparitions have taken place should be considered as sacred, as a site for pilgrimages, as a place for prayer, meditations, and worship; where all liturgical acts can be celebrated, especially the Mass and the administration of the sacraments of Reconciliation and Holy Communion, always according to the laws of the Church and the rules of the Diocese for a conjointly planned Pastoral. . .

Sense and Value of This Declaration

. . .The present case is a religious event that is admitted by human faith founded on the testimonies of witnesses and on my own testimony, this last one obviously specially authorized by the condition of pastoral guidance that belongs to a Bishop. Not to admit it does not constitute a sin against faith.

Still, anyone who acts in such a non-believing manner must examine his underlying motivations: is it prudence or a reasonable sense of criticism, is it a biased attitude or systematic negativism before all the supernatural?

With these statements I do not intend to affirm that all and each one of the apparitions that have taken place in Finca Betania are authentic. As happens in similar circumstances, here there also have been cases of simple hallucinations incited by expectation, suggestion, emotionality, and even psychological unbalance. . .

The Divine Revelation culminates in Jesus Christ. As said in the Second Vatican Council: "He with His presence and manifestation, with His words and actions, signs and miracles, above all with His death and glorious Resurrection, with the coming of the Spirit of truth, completes all the Revelation and confirms it as a divine testimony. . .Therefore another public revelation should not be expected before the glorious manifestation of

Jesus Christ Our Lord" (*Dei Verbum* 4).

In relation with the interpretation of the Revelation the Council affirms: "Tradition and Scriptures constitute the sacred depository of God's Word trusted to the Church. The job of interpreting accurately the Word of God, oral or written, has been given only to the Magisterium of the Church, which exercises it in the name of Jesus Christ" (*Dei Verbum* 10).

The previous explanation does not imply that since the death of the last Apostle, the communication of God with man ceased, or that after Jesus Christ all revelations are impossible. That would contradict the history of the Church...

Apparitions and Visions

Apparitions and visions can be referred to as constants in the history of salvation...

The apparitions and visions related in the Sacred Scriptures are numerous both in the Old and New Testaments. Hence, they are confirmed in their supernatural authenticity by divine inspiration and by the Magisterium of the Church.

From the Church's patristic origins to our days there have been numerous apparitions which have turned the history of the Church. These apparitions form part of the charismatic dimension of the Church which is conjugated with its ministerial dimension, though we have to mention that the ministerial dimension is a charism in itself...

As the Second Vatican Council expresses in its constitution, *"Lumen Gentium,"* N. 12: "...The judgment over their authenticity and over their reasonable exercise belongs to those who have authority in the Church, those who have the responsibility above all not to suffocate the

Spirit but to test it all and keep what is good" (Cfs Tes 5, 12 y 19, 21)...

In this way we can conclude that God wants Mary, our Mother in faith, who kept loyally the teachings of the divine mysteries (Cfr Luc 2, 19 y 21) and whose visit to Elizabeth was the first evangelization on the mystery of Christ (Cfr: Luc 1, 39-45), to visit the Church in these later times as evangelist in a period when faith is in crisis...

Conclusion

Ending this Pastoral Instruction I thank the Lord for He has given our Diocese and our country the privilege of the visit of Our Blessed Virgin; for in this period of our ecclesiastical history marked with a new evangelization, she encourages us to a renewal and deepening in faith, and to a projection of that faith into an integral conversion, in prayer and apostolic commitment; because in this divided world she has come as RECONCILER OF NATIONS.

Through the visit of Our Mother, may the Lord grant us that effusion of His Spirit He granted Elizabeth when Our Lady visited her. And if on that occasion Our Lady proclaimed: *"from now on all generations shall call me blessed because the Almighty has done wonders in me"* (*Luke* 1:48-49); may her intercession do wonders in the devotees piously attending the place she has chosen to manifest herself.

✠Pio Bello Ricardo
Bishop of Los Teques, November 21, 1987

Epilogue

Since the preceding book was written, we have re-interviewed Maria, and culled more of her valuable insights. In that time her health has precipitously deteriorated, making it nearly impossible, at times, to hear her words. Everyone around her is hopeful and confident that the ailment will soon end. "This test that I am going through now is very great," is all Maria says. But her mind is fully intact, and extraordinary events continue.

In 2002 Maria's beloved land of Betania was temporarily closed due to a flash flood that rose more than twenty feet in a river adjacent to the grotto. But in the end, even this was an uplifting, miraculous story. According to Carlos Marrero Bornn, the articulate, dedicated son-in-law who interprets for her, Maria foresaw the event just days before.

It began on September 22, 2002, during a family gathering. There was what Carlos, a Caracas businessman, describes as a strange sign in the sky. "It was a Sunday, and it was something incredible," he recounts. "We were at my mother-in-law's house, on the porch, and were sharing with her — having a beautiful family time — when suddenly, in the sky, in this beautiful, calm blue sky, we saw a cloud that resembled a white feather, like the feather of a dove. You can see many things in clouds, but it was so similar to a feather that we all immediately commented about it. It was *really* detailed — really something.

"My mother-in-law couldn't see, from where she was seated on her wheelchair, so we moved her and she was completely amazed. *She got goose bumps and said it was a sign that God wanted to tell her something*. She not only saw the feather, but also the face of Our Lord. We too could see some features of His face, but you could tell it was much clearer for her. She started to 'receive' — to feel in her heart — and as she was receiving, the cloud changed from the shape of a feather to different shapes while the air remained very still with no breeze. The air wasn't moving. It was very stable. But this cloud changed forms and the first thing my mother-in-law said she felt was a 'storm, a big storm coming.' And she said she didn't know how to stop it. 'I have to pray for that,' she said, 'because I see that it is going to be something very fast and unexpected. At the same time it will be not a bad thing; it will be a purification.' "

Carlos says that at first he and others speculated it might be related to a hurricane that had been roaming the Caribbean, but Maria also mentioned that "men wanted war," and so there was also speculation that the "storm" might be a metaphor for coming military conflict.

Two days later came the answer: It was a storm alright — a real deluge — and it put the famous apparition site under water.

According to Bornn, the storm nearly took the lives of a caretaker and his family. He says they were saved by hearing Maria's voice (even though the mystic was an hour away at her home in Caracas).

Recalls Bornn: "They had one daughter and a baby boy. They told us it was clear most of the night, that you couldn't have predicted a storm was coming. It started pouring at midnight and suddenly, at about three in the morning, they heard their baby crying. Henry, who is the caretaker, stood up from bed and found his legs submerged in water, almost up to the knees. He got very scared. The electrical power was off. He was desperate because he heard the river roaring. His wife started crying, holding the baby, but suddenly Henry's wife heard Maria Esperanza's voice. She said she heard my mother-in-law singing! Henry couldn't hear it, but his wife said she heard Maria."

"When Henry opened the door, Betania was under water," continues Bornn. "The river was covering everything, the current was so strong that they thought they would die. But his wife said, 'Follow me. I'm hearing Maria Esperanza's voice.' She started to follow the voice and he followed with the baby and their daughter, and they reached the top of a little hill that wasn't under the water. That's the place she felt Maria Esperanza wanted her to be."

As it turned out, it was a safe haven. They went unscathed, but the flood destroyed many surrounding homes and swept away trees. The grotto at Betania was filled with water (although, in another little miracle, the flood never touched the statue even as it altered the area's very landscape).

Betania has since recovered, but we ask: was that occurrence a harbinger?

Maria's answer: yes. Esperanza believes something new will now start in Betania, "like a rebirth," and that the world is approaching momentous times, as she has expressed previously.

"The same day that she predicted the storm, she said that in the near future there will come times in which we will need a lot of courage," notes Carlos. "We're going to have to pray a lot. She is praying that somehow war doesn't happen. These are times of big changes, in many ways for the better, a preparation for what is to come." As for timing: "From God's point of view, it is the near future, because for Him time doesn't matter. But my mother-in-law does feel many things are going to happen very, very soon, but from the human point of view the situation in the world right now is quite complicated."

What does Maria herself say most recently?

Below is a question-and-answer we compiled from personal visits and phone conversations. We'd like to mention that while you will see dialogue about her mysticism, it often pains Maria to speak about herself and her gifts. We urged her to do so for the historical record. We must also note that while Maria answered many of the questions (often speaking in a barely audible tone, at times with the help of a special microphone), Carlos, Geo, and other family members assisted, often filling in the details. It was a wide-ranging, free-wheeling series of chats, and it started with the question:

Having felt so close to Padre Pio, what was it like for you, Maria, on the day of his canonization?

For me it was very beautiful, very beautiful. It moved me deeply. Very much. I was so happy — so happy that my *joy radiated*. It was like a light coming out of me, the joy. I saw like a light and was walking with the light. I was inspired to go on, to go on walking, until my last day, until my last moment. It was a spiritual experience. I trusted that sooner or later, things will improve and I will be more able and the moment will come in which I will give the light I felt to others.

That light will enlighten all my mind, all my feelings, all my heart, and it will open my heart to the grace and put a smile on my lips, the smile of an innocent child, because innocence is the most beautiful thing. That day I had this feeling in my heart: the sensation of being an innocent child. It was a great event. I will never forget [Maria begins crying]. I felt from that moment on, my mission was to give glory to God, an extension of the mission Padre Pio had. It was so filled with hope. I felt so little. The woman that I was stayed behind and I became like an innocent child.

Geo: It was a very interesting moment. It's hard from our human point of view to understand what she was feeling inside. [During this conversation, Maria felt Padre Pio present.]

Have you seen Padre Pio since his canonization?

Yes.

Does he look different now?

No. He presents himself exactly the way he is, in a very natural way.

Maria, Padre Pio said bilocation was like an extension of his personality. What do you experience? How do you describe bilocation? Do you feel like you have actually changed locations?

Sometimes I know where I go, but other times I don't. I find out because someone sees me and tells me. This afternoon I saw myself in New York City and wanted to talk to you this afternoon. It was to tell you that I want you to hear from my lips, "May God bless you."

Do you know when a healing is taking place? Can you feel when someone is being cured?

Yes. I can feel a very strong energy coming out of me, a very strong energy that flows through me.

We know you have seen heaven. Have you also seen purgatory?

Yes.

What was it like?

It's exactly the same feeling that you have in a cemetery. It's like a cemetery filled with candles. That's the way it looks and the feeling you have when you're there – the feeling of sadness you get from a cemetery, and of loneliness.

We know Padre Pio was visited by souls from purgatory. Are you also visited by purgatorial souls?

Geo: Yes, there have been many visits from the souls in purgatory. I especially remember one occasion when my wife had the experience of going through purgatory. This was in 1973. Our Lord allowed Maria to visit purgatory, and it happened in front of a group of people. One of the souls was desperate and grabbed her hand and when Maria came out of purgatory, she found her hand was burned — like when you get burned by hot water, with like a red spot on her hand that hurt. But in the end it was very beautiful because the soul was saved. This soul told Maria her name, and it turned out to be a Venezuelan girl that our daughter, Maria Coromoto, knew.

Maria also saw many other souls who extended their arms asking for help, as if in desperation. This girl had the chance to grab Maria and told her she was from Caracas. "Please help me," she said, as she grabbed the little finger and palm on my wife's right hand. Because of that impression, Maria started to pray for her every day, and one day she felt the soul was released from purgatory. It was very moving. Maria said the soul would give a sign when she was released from purgatory, and the day Maria felt this girl's release, a tree that was at our house — like a dry tree, in hibernation — suddenly bloomed.

When Maria saw it, it was filled with white flowers. It had been dry, nearly dead, or hibernating, and now it was blooming. It was a sign from the girl in purgatory. It was beautiful. Real flowers from a dry tree!

How many times has Maria been taken to purgatory? Many times?

Geo: Only that one time.

Have the souls ever visited your home?

Geo: There are so many cases, but Maria doesn't always know if they have been in purgatory. In my opinion, most of the souls are not in purgatory. They are wandering. They are stuck, tied to what they left behind. They are wandering around the world without having a place to stay. There have been spirits that came close to Maria, spirits that seemed like they were destroyed, devastated. They had been wandering in like *space* and as they got closer to Maria, she couldn't see them as recognizable figures, but as shades, like amorphous forms without shape, and suddenly when Maria started praying for them, these amorphous forms recovered their human form, and thanks to prayer, started to rise to the Light. That's the way special people from God have the grace to help all those souls without light — lost souls. It's an important mission — to get close to the Light of God.

I'm not sure of the exact year, but in a message from God the Father to Maria about ten or 15 years ago, He said that it was very important to pray for the souls in purgatory because we cannot imagine how great their suffering is. From that moment on, we have prayed the 100 Requiem every Monday: "God give them eternal rest, give to the souls eternal rest." You pray that a hundred times.

Diverting a bit onto other issues of life: Maria, did you know early in life how many children you would have?

Our Lord told me I would have six roses and a bud. That meant six girls and one boy.

Did you feel specially instructed as to what to name them?

Yes, all of them, and I also knew when I was pregnant, and when I was ready to have the baby.

What saints are especially close to you at present, in addition to Padre Pio? Who are you praying to in the current times?

There are many that I pray to, although lately I have been thinking, in a special way, of Josemarie Escriva, the founder of Opus Dei. But I pray to all the saints.

That time that St. Therese "threw" you the rose: Did she actually throw it, or was it more like it suddenly materialized in your hand?

I saw St. Therese the Little Flower throwing the rose. I saw it flying and grabbed it.

As far as saints who have appeared to you, Maria, which are they, who has been the most memorable, in addition to saints like the Blessed Mother, St. Therese, St. Joseph, and St. Padre Pio?

St. Ignatius of Loyola, Anthony Mary Claret, and Mother Cabrini also come frequently — as well as St. John Bosco. Also, St. Mary Mazzarello and St. Peter the Apostle, St. Francis of Assisi, and St. Paul. St. Peter has spoken to me many times.

What about Mother Cabrini? You have a very special devotion to her. Why?

I heard about her when I was a little girl and the first time I traveled to New York, it was thanks to Mother Cabrini, because she promised me, spiritually, that she would take me there. From that moment we began a close relationship. Spiritually, she is my godmother. The first message that I received from her was in *English*.

Carlos: You must see this message. It is in English [which Maria doesn't speak], but in Maria's handwriting and everything!

Geo: I have a file of the main messages on their original paper. Many I typed with a typewriter. More than half are in original handwriting and are treasures, written on everything you can imagine: napkins and everything. She received messages in restaurants, on the street, everywhere.

Were your parents very devout, Maria?

Yes. My father was a merchant. His name was Aniceto Medrano and my mother's was Filomena Parra de Medrano. My father used to buy and sell merchandise: cattle, coffee, everything. The Indians called him "dad" because he supplied them with many things they needed. There were three boys and two girls, including me. One of them wanted to be a priest and studied in the seminary but then quit.

Switching gears once more, we wonder: It is said you had visions pertaining to the year 2004, which for some readers, by the time they see this, will have come and gone, even though, as we speak, it is 2003. Might those visions of 2004 have been tied to the Eucharistic Congress the Pope recommended for that year? And might they have also relate to further study on the Blessed Mother, which the Pope also requested specifically for 2004? Is there a connection?

Yes. The Eucharist. This is very important. I have daily Eucharist and this is very important — nourishment.

[Turning to Carlos.] **Now, Maria has had the Eucharistic miracle where a Host actually appears on her tongue. What was that like, Carlos? Did you not witness this?**

Carlos: Yes. And it was one of the most incredible experiences of my whole life. We were in my mother-in-law's house, in her room, and were talking. She was planning what to cook that day. And suddenly she said, "Oh, Carlos, you know what? Maybe today we're going to have a very special lunch." Suddenly she fell on her knees and I wasn't expecting that, so I thought something was wrong, that it was related to her health, and I got scared. But there was a smile on her face that told me that it was not something bad. Suddenly she opened her mouth and there was nothing on her tongue. But then, boom, the Host appeared on her tongue. I saw like a tiny white dot but then, boom, it turned into a huge Host.

I was overwhelmed by that experience and I fell on my knees. She started signaling me, like hurrying me to call the rest, and I called all the members of the family who were there and they all came to her room and you could smell bread and wine all over the room.

It was amazing and it wasn't only one Host. Suddenly she closed her mouth as if to swallow the one that appeared on her tongue, and when she opened her mouth there was another Host, and then another. At the end she received a message from Our Lord in which He told her that the Hosts were for all the ones who were not receiving daily Communion. It wasn't only that time. It has happened many times to her.

Maria, in that instance, did you feel an angel was giving you Communion, or the Lord Himself?

I believe it is an angel. At the beginning there were angels, bringing me the spiritual Communion. But the day of the many Hosts, I received a message from Our Lord and I suppose He was giving me the Hosts because He gave the message on receiving for those who did not receive. But at the beginning there were angels.

What is the greatest need in the Church right now?

The Church right now needs holy priests. That's what it needs.

How do you think the Church will come out of its current crisis?

It will come out okay, even though there are many obstacles. God is so great. He is perfect. He won't allow His children to perish nor be weakened, no matter what happens. God is perfect and I trust and wait for the storm to pass and then everything will take its place. It's the way it has to be, because Our Lord is touching hearts and making them young, in order to be able to appreciate what youth means. He is just and He wants to save us all.

How do you feel about the new mysteries of the Rosary, the Luminous Mysteries? Why do you think the Pope installed them?

Whatever the Pope does is great for me. It's just perfect for me.

But Maria, why do you think the Pope installed those new mysteries?

Because Our Lord dictated them to him. I feel He dictated them.

There was a man, a priest, who was recently beatified, and they say he came up with the idea in 1957.

Yes, but Our Lord is the One Who told the Pope to do it, to come out with the new mysteries. Our Lord told the Pope.

Does the Pope see Our Blessed Mother?

[Maria smiles] He will never say.

Is the Pope in danger?

He is in danger but he has great assistance. Our Lady is always with him, protecting him. Our Lady herself is covering him with her mantle. She loves him very much — very much.

When you referred to 2004, were you referring to something in the spiritual realm or here on earth?

In both, Michael. Like parallel. The spiritual and material realms. It's something that cannot be avoided. It cannot be stopped. It is the beginning of something.

When you see a recovery beginning in 2004, does that mean an end of disasters, or that the purification will continue?

Geo: Maria feels there will be a change in people. We will achieve new innocence, a new spiritual state.

Was there anything about your earliest years, before St. Therese appeared to you, Maria, that indicated your spiritual gifts?

The Lord appeared to me once before and once after. His eyes were blue and He had a long beard and was wearing a robe that fell on His arms. He came like a soft wind, surrounding me, and under my feet, it was like the ground was trembling. It was something very big and beautiful. Just thinking of it makes me shake, makes me tremble. I had a similar experience with God the Father in 1968 at my house in Valle Arriba. The house was in front of the French embassy. I loved that house very much. It was a very special house. I felt a very strong spiritual aspect there, a force. I went out of my house, to the garden, one day, and felt that I had to open my arms. That time, I opened my arms and I started shaking, and the Lord, God the Father and the Son together, told me, "*Here you have this beautiful home. From here you have been able to do whatever you wish.*

But now, My daughter, I want you to renounce everything and go to Rome. I want you to spend some years with your family there," and that's what happened. We left for Rome. God's power is so immense that it makes your heart beat a lot faster, but after that the peace that comes is so deep that you feel a total surrender.

If at that time I had to die, it would have been perfect. After being in tune with God, death is perfect. It goes in perfect harmony. But it makes me feel embarrassed to discuss these things, because sometimes they are not easy to understand. Everyone said, are you crazy, you're going to leave this beautiful home, but I didn't care.

What happened next as far as apparitions? Who came next?

After that came a period of silence. The period of my childhood was like a preparation for my mission, but in a silent way. At that age and the following years, I had the gift of seeing people and reading their souls. I knew what they were feeling. In those years, during the night, I used to awaken and my mother would come and sit down on my bed and hold my hand and asked me what happened, why I was awake. I used to tell her, "I am here talking with St. Therese." She was like my sister. I felt her that way. She used to talk to me in a very natural fashion. It makes me embarrassed to talk about this. She was a companion to me, like my little best friend. She used to awaken me to go to Mass. She used to come to tell me, "*Go to Mass. It's time to go to Mass.*" I love St. Therese in such a deep way.

Did you go to Mass every day as a child?

There was a woman named Maria de Lourdes who used to take care of me and when I was a child, she took me to the 6 a.m. Mass every day. I learned that in life we are to become strong and robust. It's not really important, where the pain or joy is. The important thing is to have a conscience and to do what's right, what God wants you to do. I have always had that in my mind, since I was a little child: my mission, and my fear of God. I have never wanted to offend anyone. I was a shy child. And I wanted to become a nun. After my childhood passed, when I was a young lady, I spent a lot of time with nuns. I felt so loved by them. I was like a little sister to them. The Mother Superior told me that no matter what happened, I would be a part of the convent, and that I would have a place there spiritually. It was in that Franciscan convent where St. Therese again appeared to me and said that God didn't want me to be a nun, but to sacrifice myself as a wife and mother.

You say that you were young when you first began to "read souls." What is reading souls like? How do you see a person's entire life?

It's like a movie. I see all the images from the past of a person, the present, and the future, like a movie.

That day you were healed as a youngster, and there was the shaking: could you give us some more details?

Actually it was at a home. I saw Jesus dressed in His white robe. He was carrying like a letter or small book in His Hands.

What were some other significant events in your life?

Geo: An occurrence in August of 1954 was one of the most significant moments of her life. Maria was praying with a group of friends in her house. She was seated praying the Rosary and suddenly they heard a noise, a loud sound, and saw a light from the ceiling. A ray of light came from the ceiling and hit Maria hard, struck her chest. At that moment she had a very sharp pain and lost consciousness.

She was two or three days in bed, like immobilized. Later she started to recover. What struck her heart appeared days later, materialized in the form of an object like the point of an arrow or sword, a very strange metal. It came out of her chest. On the sharp object was something written. It said, "Heaven, earth, new life," and it had a little dry blood on it. She kept it wrapped in cotton.

Have there been other objects, besides the roses, that have come from her body?

Geo: No. One time she was operated on for her left knee. She went to surgery and they removed like a lump or cyst. The doctor was very amazed because while he was operating, suddenly, on the screen they use over part of the body, he saw the image of Our Lady and called the nurse. He also called the director of the hospital. And he knew nothing about Maria. He said it was the most amazing surgery he had done, because there was no blood from the incision. She didn't bleed at all. It was the cleanest operation he had ever done. That was in 1987.

When Padre Pio was your confessor, Maria, did he give advice on your spiritual gifts?

He asked me to be very prudent because people are always looking for scandal and there are persecutions. I was surrounded by many people at that time in my life, people who followed me, and he advised me to be very humble and low-profile.

Could you see angels around Padre Pio?

It makes me feel embarrassed...

That's okay. Don't feel embarrassed.

For me it is like a lack of humility.

Geo: With Padre Pio, she would hear him spiritually. We used to go back and forth to San Giovanni. They could have done the same in Rome [communicated without actually meeting], but he wanted Maria to go to San Giovanni.

How many times did you meet with Padre Pio?

Geo: At least twenty.

Did you see him alone?

Geo: Usually it was in the confessional, or in the sacristy. There we had the chance to be with him two or three times. The first time we went as a family, with our first two daughters. They sat us on the altar and Padre Pio came out of the confessional and he placed his hands on Maria's head and my head and on the children and he told me, "Behave well, behave well." Maria had gone to see him before this.

The first time he spoke to you, what did Padre Pio say, Maria?

It makes me feel embarrassed...

Did you see anything around Padre Pio that was unusual, unlike what you see around others?

The extraordinary thing about him was his humility and his

simplicity. It was something that immediately moved you and reached your heart, your soul, your mind. A communication started immediately. It was like talking without words. Since then, he has been following me.

What else do you recall about Padre Pio?

Geo: There was a family we knew and they were spiritual children of Padre Pio and he would ring their doorbell. He would ring the doorbells of his spiritual children at four o'clock in the morning, to unite with them in prayer.

You heard this also? Would your doorbell ring?

Yes, we have heard it, but it wasn't continual. This family we knew, the Collis, for them it was every morning. Padre Pio told them personally — the mother, Josepina Colli — that from America, from South America, would come a girl and that they had to help her, a young woman, and she would have many children and she would have to help her with her children [indicating that this woman was Maria].

When you were still single, did you see Padre Pio alone, one to one, Maria?

I was alone with him twice. I remember one time I was sleeping and Padre Pio began calling me in my dream.

The day he died, didn't he come to you and say he was there to say good-bye?

Yes.

Did he say anything else?

He said, "I will always be with you." And he has never separated from me.

This was in a chapel?

Geo: Yes, in a chapel in our house. We were celebrating a Mass in the house. Many of those Maria knows come to say good-bye when they die, and the same happened with Padre Pio.

The phenomenon of glitter. This happens at Betania and to people associated with Betania. What does it mean?

Some is golden, but I don't know what it means.

When the Virgin Mary appeared for the first time at Betania, was that out of a cloud or out of fire?

She came out of a cloud.

What about Venezuela? It has been going through quite a crisis. What will happen?

I see sadness in the near future, sadness and tears. But it will pass.

When you had a vision of smoke coming out of the World Trade Center in the early 1990s, was that related to the first attack on the World Trade Center in 1993, or to the second attack on September 11?

It related to the second one.

Did you "see" the buildings fall?

The whole thing, yes, the smoke and the shaking. When I had the vision I felt the shaking, and in those days, after the vision, I felt very affected and depressed, and I went there in the spirit for many days, for weeks, at [what would become] Ground Zero, praying. What God wants to be revealed in that place are twin churches. Two churches that resemble the towers but are churches, built there. That's what God really wants. I know it's impossible, and it's a shame, but you never know.

Throughout the Bible are accounts of towers that fell when mankind made them into idols. Do you think the World Trade Center was the idol of money?

Yes.

Do you think men have learned anything from it or that we are just going back to the way we were?

They are heading to the same direction again. They want to go back to what they had. God wants two churches, twin churches, to be built there to save the world, because if they do that, if they build them, there would be many souls saved and the world would be saved — if they build two churches in that place.

Carlos: This is not the first time she has said this. She said this back on September 11 — churches for those of all faiths. It would be a lesson for the whole world. She says this would even do more economic good because people would come from all over to pay their respects.

Let's jump around a bit. Here's a question. Why are evil spirits so active now?

There is very little time for the devil. Very little time.

Is the unification of Europe good — or will it lead to an evil world government?

I see too much confusion in the unification of Europe. I see a lot of confusion.

You've warned about Iraq, the war. What do you see as the dangers? What could Iraq lead to? What would it cause?

It would be a crazy thing to do, to attack Iraq, because they will attack and attack and attack, and they are prepared. They are just waiting to respond. They are just waiting for something little to fall upon, the terrorists and Iraq together. Leaders must be humble in heart and very wise, with patience and generosity. We are here in this world to serve — serve, serve, serve, and never get tired of serving. We can never allow ourselves to be provoked. We have to be balanced. We must always have our minds on Heaven. We are here today because God wants us to be here.

For now, God is holding back the arms of terrorists with His right arm. If we pray and honor Him, He will stop everything. Right now He is stopping things because of Our Lady. She is involved in many things to defeat the enemy, and this moment needs a lot of peace. Injustice is reigning right now, but Our Lord is fixing everything. Anyone who dares do something, who rises to do evil, will pay the consequences. Instead we must raise our hearts and open our eyes to the infinite, to eternity, and say only, "My God, my Lord, we're waiting for you!"

Will America find itself lessened in stature, diminished in the future?

The U.S. is very smart and intelligent. It has many talents. It is a nation that does what is just. But it is also a nation that must go back to God.

We are speaking in early 2003. There is still major danger from terrorists, is there not?

The risk is still there. You have to be alert all the time

because there may be surprises. *The United States must be very careful right now.*

Back to the Church and it's crisis...

I feel this whole situation will lead to a difficult moment, a very strong confrontation. We must be very serene. And we must be very humble — humility. It will end in a strong, difficult confrontation. The north against the south, the east against the west...

This is in the context of the Church or —?

War. Mankind must change. From this moment on, there has to come a change, because there are the pretentious ones who want to lead us toward destruction. There are many who want change. But the ones who are leading us today are too arrogant and they are guiding us toward problems. Prayer will be our salvation. *Prayer.* The four pillars are prayer, meditation, penance, and the Eucharist.

Again, what about the crisis with priests in the Church?

We have to pray as never before, with all our hearts. As many times as possible, say: "My Lord, my God, my Lord, my God" for the intentions of the Church.

What is the future of Betania?

The city of God.

Large, or small and humble?

It will stay simple and small. But many people will come, many children, many, many children and youth, young people.

Maria, what about Jesus, and the way He might come?

It is very different than what people think. He's going to come in silence, because otherwise He would be killed again. People will realize He is among us little by little. I'm seeing Him right now. He has His mantle covering His hair. He has a robe like white and black. His first presentation will be like this, because in those days an innocent person whom He loves a lot will die, an innocent person. This will shock the world, will move the world. Many people will believe. He will disappear for some days and appear again. And when He disappears, people will go back again to the mess, to the crazed things. He will bilocate, He will multiply Himself, to assist everyone, in their homes, because this will be a definite thing. He will come and knock on every door. And then people will realize it is truly Him. He will let Himself be seen for a little while and then will disappear until God decrees what has to be done. And then people will understand what is happening and begin preparing themselves. There is not much time for that. I will say from ten to twenty years. Everything is already in place, in motion. I see palm trees, and they will say again, "Blessed is He Who comes in the Name of the Lord." We are being prepared right now. I know what I am saying sounds crazy, but I have to say what I have to say. Sometimes I am like St. Thomas, who has to put his finger in His side.

Geo: See *Psalm* 71. It is very clear there.

Are you speaking of visions, or maybe dreams? That Christ will return in visions? We look at *Matthew* 24 and *Luke* 21 and it says when He comes again it will be in glory on a cloud. So you're speaking of a manifestation — not the Second Coming?

The same way He resurrected, that is how God is going to appear to you, to me, in that way, the same way as He resurrected, as an apparition. That's the way He is going to appear, to you, to me, to everyone in that way. He is going to start appearing. He already is among us but is not letting us see Him. With our brains, in this physical reality, we can only see what God wants us to see, but it only needs a little touch from God to open another little door in our brains to see Jesus whenever He wants us to see Him. That's why I have been saying to be ready, because things are starting to happen.

The Catechism says the Second Coming is followed by the end of the world. How do you respond to that?

Geo: It is an interpretation. Read *Psalm* 71. When He comes in glory is the Final Judgment, the end of this world. If He comes now, the ones who will receive Him will be the Pope and all the faithful souls in the world, no one else, because they are expecting Him and waiting for Him. We are also waiting.

Has the Pope ever bilocated to you, Maria? Do you speak to Him in your mind?

Carlos: I have two testimonies of this myself. Last year, after September 11, he came to Maria while we were in her room. It was close to midnight and suddenly I heard her speaking in Italian. The Pope and Maria spoke in Italian. After that experience he appeared to my mother-in-law in her room again. My father-in-law and I were talking to her and suddenly she started smiling and said, "The Holy Father is with us. Kneel." She said he was standing right there and giving her courage to go on. She saw him perfectly.

Do you think the anti-christ is alive in the world right now?

[Maria declines comment]

What does the spinning sun mean?

The sun spinning is like a warning, like an alert.

When you see angels, Maria, how do they usually appear to you?

Like children, with little wings. As soon as they see me, they open their wings like waving and moving around very fast.

You see them with your eyes open, or with your soul?

With my eyes open.

Do they also come in human form?

Whenever they present themselves as human beings, even though they are angels, I treat them like human beings.

Geo, what was the date of the first rose coming out of Maria, and what was it like?

Geo: It always happens the same way. Some hours before, Maria begins to feel bad, weak, like a general malaise. The first time and all the rest happened the same way. She sat down and started to feel a very strong pain in her chest, on the side of her heart. She breathed with difficulty. She opened her blouse and from the middle of the chest between the two breasts it started to grow, a fresh rose, with little drops of water, of dew. The bishop studied the case and tried to research any saint who had the same phenomenon. But there was not one exactly like this. There was one with a rose that came out of his mouth.

But that first time: It must have been a shock. What were the circumstances?

Geo: It was a *huge* shock. It happened in our house in Betania. It was January 18, 1986. The last was August 15, 1995, and it was also in Betania. It was videotaped.

What was Maria doing when it happened? What were the circumstances?

For the whole day she was having the malaise. The pain in her heart started, and it was very sharp. One time it happened at Betania in front of two physicians. They were examining her.

That first time, what did you do? Did you take her to a doctor?

She was sitting on a chair in the chapel in the house. She wanted to go to the chapel.

Do you associate the rose with any saint, or an angel? Who does it, Maria, who causes the rose manifestation — is it St. Therese the Little Flower?

At that moment, my mind is blank. Everything is white.

You are in such touch with the supernatural, and with angels. What about speaking to our guardian angels?

We nourish them with our daily prayers.

As far as miracles, why specifically the place called Betania? Why Medjugorje? Why Fatima? Why certain locations?

Because of the lack of humility in the big cities. The Lord chooses as He chooses.

We learn in these conversations that you met twice in Venezuela with Mother Teresa of Calcutta, when she was on visits. As we understand it, during one visit you spent hours together because her plane was delayed and you stayed all night with her as she waited for her delayed flight. Did you pray a lot together?

Geo: Everything was prayer. We took the chance [while waiting for the next flight] to visit one of Mother Teresa's houses in Caracas, and when we did we had the chance to kneel down and pray altogether for about an hour. Then we took her back to the airport. The plane was supposed to take off at midnight but took off at five a.m. This was in 1982.

Maria, has Mother Teresa appeared to you since she died?

[No comment]

Geo: Many times she has spoken to my wife.

And what about Betania? What more can we say about this place?

Geo: When I first met my wife, she was given messages, that a piece of land would be given to us for a very big reason. It is land that has been chosen from a long time ago, prepared by God.

Was the grotto there already?

The waterfall was there, but the grotto was constructed later.

What was the history of the land? Who owned it?

Geo: An evangelist. He was the owner before we bought the land, and they used to baptize people in the river, immersing them. He was a lawyer. His name was Dr. Perez.

An evangelist! That's very interesting...

Later I described the apparition to him and told him we saw Our Lady. And after I gave my testimony, he said, "Okay, if you're going to build a town on that land, I have to have my house there also!"

Was he operating a sugar plantation?

Yes. He sold sugar cane. And he gave it the name "Betania." One of the first manifestations of the power of the place, before Our Lady appeared, after we got the land, was a person who was driving from the countryside and passing Betania when suddenly he saw a rosary above the land — *a huge rosary*. He was a Catholic. The rosary was all lighted, not a formation of clouds. A complete rosary in light! He told the experience to the bishop.

What about the butterfly that is seen? What more can we learn about that?

Geo: In a message that Maria received from Our Lady, the Blessed Mother told Maria that in Betania, "I will make myself be known in the form of a butterfly."

Carlos: The butterfly has played with the kids. She flies around them, at Betania and also at my mother-in-law's house.

Geo: Sometimes you will see it in the street, as you're driving on the highway. Whenever it appears we pray the *Hail Mary*. That's a sign, when you see her in the street, that Our Lady is with you, is protecting you. It appears and disappears in the same way. Not like a *pop*, but just that you don't see it anymore.

Turning now to Samir, who is with us this day, another son-in-law. We understand you had extraordinary experiences at Betania. What happened?

Samir: It was the first time I came to Betania. I had a friend who used to tell me about Maria Esperanza, and I decided to go. I waited almost six hours until 3:30 in the afternoon. We crossed the river, carried Maria across the river — there wasn't a bridge back then — and anyway, that day, she started praying the Rosary, and when we approached the grotto, all of a sudden she showed us a light — how a light from the sun in the woods was forming an image like Our Lady of Guadalupe. I saw it myself in the wood, and I'm a scientist! After that, petals began appearing on Maria's hands. And she received a message from Our Lady — about praying for the young and for those with drug problems. After that she felt that she should approach the river, and pick up a stone, and that's what she did. I accompanied her to the river and she took a stone, a heavy gray stone, right out of the water — and when she took it she felt something on the bottom and was afraid, so she turned it up — and when she opened her left hand Our Lady of Guadalupe, like we had seen in the wood, was exactly there in like a plastic or ceramic material stuck on the stone, and the smell of roses was very strong.

It was "attached" to the stone?

It was attached like an object that had stuck to the stone. It had been under the water, and at first when Maria felt it, she was afraid. But the amazing thing was the smell of roses. This was 1986. I also saw when she received the Eucharist, where Maria Esperanza would open her mouth and you can see the Eucharist wet, not the exact shape because of the saliva. One time we were going outside to get into the car and Maria knelt, opened her mouth, and there was like a wind blowing. And I saw several Eucharists appear miraculously on her tongue, like five or six Eucharists all in a stack. The last Eucharist had a Roman-style cross on it. They were typical size, stacked on her tongue. We had been on the way to the supermarket.

Turning to you, Coromoto: as a daughter, you must have seen so much. Didn't you have an experience where rose petals began flowing out of the pocket of a jacket you had borrowed from your mother?

Coromoto: We were invited to a conference in Tampa in February of 1994 and were getting ready to go when I asked my mother for a jacket. We left, and when we got to the conference, my mother started to talk, gave her speech. I had the jacket on, and a nametag with my name written. While my mother was talking, I felt something [moving] inside the jacket. At first I thought it might be an insect. It felt like it was pulsating, or tickling, like popcorn was popping. I saw in the nameplate, like caught in it, a *petal.* It was stuck. And while I was feeling this sensation of movement in the pocket, I put my hand in the pocket and I saw the petals coming out and out and out — multiplying inside the pocket.

So they just kept coming out?

Coromoto: I was just amazed, and everyone started seeing it — dozens and dozens of petals.

This went on for how long?

Coromoto: Like five minutes or longer.

Maria Gracie: Another time, when we opened the washing machine, there were all these petals all over my mother's clothes. It was so amazing!

Carlos: We are accustomed to this now.

Coromoto: My mother is always giving us a new surprise. The supernatural became like natural.

But is there anything that especially sticks out, that you especially remember?

Coromoto: Yes. One time my mother was giving a blessing. She used to have the Rosary every Friday. And when she gave the blessing — to all the people who were there — she was *lifted*.

"Lifted"? Like levitated?

Coromoto: Yes. I was five years old or so and looking up and it was, "Whoa, my mother is floating!"

How far was she off the floor?

Coromoto: Like this [indicating two or so feet].

For a while, or just a moment?

Coromoto: For a while. And every Good Friday, she started having oil from her hands and her face, with a beautiful perfume. She would breathe on you and you could smell like oil with roses.

Samir: There was also oil from a picture of Jesus as a fisherman in Maria's house.

Carlos: The image poured oil for months. My mother-in-law used to clean it with pieces of cotton.

Were there other images that oiled?

Carlos: There was one of Our Lady of Fatima, and it cried one time.

Speaking of sorrow, speaking of the Blessed Mother weeping, perhaps these are omens. Take your own homeland. Many things have happened in Venezuela. Several years ago, a horrible storm killed tens of thousands not far from Caracas due to mudslides. Horrible. And now the nation has been in the midst of tremendous turmoil, with banks closed and violent political protests. Why is this happening? Why Venezuela?

Samir: Maria used to say that "[God's] justice will start in Venezuela."

Mercy. Justice. Winding down here, just some last questions. Maria, when you see the Virgin, is it more like an ethereal vision, or is it like she is actually a person, of flesh and blood?

I have seen her both ways. Ethereal and like I am seeing you right now.

Wasn't there a time when she took you into her arms or you sat on her lap?

Geo: It was the month of September, 1988. It happened in Sardinia.

Carlos: I remember the story. My mother-in-law was sleeping and suddenly she saw the Baby Jesus. She didn't know it was the Baby Jesus. She saw a boy, like a 12-year-old, who entered the room and signaled her to follow. As she followed him to a balcony, she saw Our Lady seated in a chair and extending her arms to her, and from that moment Maria felt like she was a little girl. Our Lady sat my mother-in-law on her lap and gave her a message.

Geo: She wrote the message and it was filed.

Maria, what does the Virgin Mary feel like?

Like a mother. At the moment I see her, my personality disappears.

Geo: I was sleeping, but when I woke up Maria told me the whole thing. She was in total emotion — very joyful and happy. She said, "Our Lady came and gave a message." Whenever she receives a message, it's always as if it is the first time. She gets excited. She never gets used to it. She always shows a great deal of joy and happiness. And each message somehow always shows a beautiful part of God's project, and brings a sensation of His great plans. With my wife there is a huge beautiful project, and it hasn't been accomplished in its greatest part yet. The messages that she has received in all these fifty years have been always to prepare her and the group that surrounds her. She has to prepare a group and this hasn't yet been explained. *The important thing has always been to prepare souls*, and this preparation is not complete, but it is for something very important that is going to happen somewhere in the future. The concept of the Betania apparition is to be prepared to enter into spiritual action and spread God's Name in every way.

Other Books By Michael H. Brown

For these other books by Michael Brown, contact him directly at www.spiritdaily.com

Secrets of the Eucharist

The continuous True Presence of Christ with us in the Blessed Sacrament is good news worth sharing! This book of heartfelt reflections on the Holy Eucharist demonstrates that devotion to this profound sacrament is fundamental to our faith. 96pp.

Seven Days with Mary

This is a book of devotion based on the most ancient and solid of Mary's apparitions. Taking one of Mary's approved appearances for each day of the week, Michael Brown explains its often hidden aspects and offers prayers and meditations to accompany it. 112 pp.

Witness - Josyp Terelya
Autobiography of Josyp Terelya
Co-Authored by Michael Brown

The dynamic autobiography of a contemporary mystic, suffering servant, and victim of Communism. Published before dramatic changes in Europe and the Soviet Union, it is a story of supernatural events and accurate predications. 344pp.

Prayer of the Warrior

A riveting account of frontline action in the eternal battle between good and evil as experienced by Michael Brown. 256 pp.

BETANIA PUBLICATIONS

Betania Publications was established to spread information about the life of Maria Esperanza Medrano de Bianchini, mystic and visionary in Betania, Venezuela. She was born on November 22, 1928 and died on August 7, 2004.

The first project of Betania Publications is the printing ~ in English and Spanish ~ of two very popular books: Michael Brown's TheBridgeto*H*eaven and Sr. Margaret Catherine Sim's Betania Apparitions.

In the future Betania Publications will publish books on Maria Esperanza's life, chaplets of prayer written by Maria Esperanza and her prophetic messages. We will produce music CD's of the acclaimed Betania Choir and DVD's about Betania and Maria Esperanza.

For More Information on Betania Publications:

Betania I
Caracas, Venezuela
[58-212] 963-7264
www.mariaesperanza.org

Betania II
One Marian Way
Medway, MA 02053
[508]533-5377
www.mariancommunity.org